For Mum,

Happy Birthday

2006

This Birding Life

This Birding Life

The Best of the *Guardian*'s Birdwatch

STEPHEN MOSS

*The*Guardian

First published 2006 by
Aurum Press Ltd, 25 Bedford Avenue, London WC1B 3AT
www.aurumpress.co.uk

in association with Guardian Books.
Guardian Books is an imprint of Guardian Newspapers Ltd.

The pieces collected in this book were first published in the *Guardian*.

Illustrations by Jan Wilczur

A catalogue record for this book is available from the British Library.

ISBN-10: 1 84513 180 0
ISBN-13: 978 1 84513 180 7

1 3 5 7 9 10 8 6 4 2
2006 2008 2010 2009 2007

Designed and typeset in Fournier by M Rules

Printed and bound in Great Britain by
Creative Print and Design, Ebbw Vale

For my late mother, Kay Moss, with fond memories of walking across a golf course on the Isles of Scilly, during a howling gale, to see Buff-breasted Sandpipers.

And for my wife Suzanne, who has not yet had that pleasure.

Contents

Introduction

O nce in a while, I try to picture what my life would have been like if I had never become interested in birds. Yet birds form such a central part of my existence, and have influenced the course of so many aspects of my life, that the idea that I might not be totally fascinated by them is, quite simply, unimaginable.

That doesn't mean that I am some sad obsessive whose every waking hour is spent thinking about, pursuing or watching birds. I have many other interests, a loving family and a wide circle of friends, most of whom are not birders themselves. But birds are always 'there' – something I can't help noticing, watching and thinking about.

Moreover, I am one of those very lucky people for whom my consuming passion is also my work: both in my job as a producer at the BBC Natural History Unit and as the author of various articles and books on birds. But for the first decade or so of my working life things were very different. The catalyst that led to the convergence of my hobby and my career came in the early 1990s, when I was working for the BBC's now defunct Continuing Education Department in London.

I had produced a now long-forgotten television series on the British weather and, together with my friend and colleague Paul Simons, had written a book to accompany it. As a result, we both began contributing short articles on the weather to the *Guardian*, commissioned by Tim Radford. A year or so later, I suggested to Tim's colleague Celia Locks that the time might be right to launch a column on birdwatching. My first 'Birdwatch' column was published in January 1993, and since then I have delivered more than 150 monthly missives, totalling over 80,000 words.

This volume contains a selection of those pieces, rearranged into chapters with common themes. I have edited them as lightly as possible, removing the odd error (mine), the occasional misprint (the *Guardian*'s), and at my editor's behest, pruned the text of clichés. But otherwise they stand more or less as they were written.

They cover a wide range of subjects: from nostalgic trips down memory lane, to memorable people, places and, of course, birding experiences – both at home and abroad. What they have in common is a consistent approach to birds and birding: a philosophy, if you like, by which I incorporate the pastime into my daily life. Like so many people, I find enjoyment, solace and quite literally 're-creation' in the experience of watching birds, whether in my back garden or the most exotic foreign location.

If I have conveyed even a little of the enormous pleasure, joy and fulfilment watching birds has brought to my life, I shall have succeeded. If you are not a birder, and these pieces persuade you to give it a go, I promise you won't regret it!

Prologue

JUNE 1998

I t's over 35 years since I began watching birds. OK, so I was only a toddler when I started, but in biblical terms, that's more than half a lifetime.

In *Fever Pitch*, Nick Hornby's celebrated book about supporting Arsenal Football Club, he wonders how many childhood pastimes you're still enjoying when you reach middle age. Playing with Lego? Only when the kids absolutely insist. Wearing short trousers? Only when I travel abroad and really let my hair down. Making up complicated fantasy games and losing myself in another world? Not as often as I'd like.

So why do I still pick up a pair of binoculars and a book of coloured pictures, and go out into the countryside to watch small, feathered creatures? It's not as if I don't have better things to do: piles of urgent tasks at work and home, and the whole multitude of distractions and entertainments available to late twentieth-century man.

Perhaps that's why I enjoy watching birds. In an ever-changing world, it provides a stability and continuity hard to find elsewhere. Indeed, it occurred to me recently that when I'm watching a particular bird, it often brings to mind the many other times I've seen that species.

For example, a lone Jackdaw just flew past my window. Seeing that bird reminded me of one afternoon a few years ago, in Galilee, in the north of Israel. I stood in the gathering dusk, in the heart of the Hula Valley, waiting for a spectacular roost of more than 20,000 cranes to pass overhead. Suddenly, I heard a familiar call: a harsh 'chack', multiplied many times. The sound came from a flock of almost a thousand Jackdaws, feeding in a lush, irrigated field. Until that moment, I didn't even know this species lived in Israel, let alone gathered there in such vast numbers.

Closing my eyes, I remembered all the other times and places I'd heard Jackdaws call, or watched as ragged black silhouettes swept across the sky. A Gloucestershire village on New Year's Day, when it was the very first bird I saw that year. The tower of an ancient Norfolk church, with a flock of Jackdaws angrily mobbing a passing Osprey. And a service station on the M4, where Rooks and Jackdaws gathered to scavenge morsels of food dropped by passing motorists.

I have a photograph of me as a toddler, aged 18 months or so, my hand outstretched to a bird. It was a tame Jackdaw, and I remember my mother telling me that it had turned up in our garden sometime back in late 1961. For a few months, it hung around to be fed, and then disappeared. Later on she showed me the photograph, and the image stuck in my mind.

Looking back, I suppose this Jackdaw was the first bird I ever looked at. Did this chance encounter, together with a child's curiosity, lead to a lifetime's all-consuming obsession with birds? Or did I throw it a piece of bread, turn away, and go off to play with my toys? I don't know. But I do know that whenever I see a Jackdaw, half a lifetime's worth of memories rise to the surface.

CHAPTER I

Growing up

1963–1982

The pieces in this chapter are a selection of my childhood birding experiences. Starting in the south-west London suburbs – in those days known as Middlesex – they cover the two places that really got me hooked on birds: the gravel-pits at Shepperton and the reservoirs at Staines.

They continue through family summer holidays, and my first tentative trips as a teenager – made with Daniel, my schoolmate, dear friend and birding companion for the past four decades. The chapter ends with a memorable trip I made to the Shetland Isles after leaving university – a trip which, looking back a quarter of a century on, I now realise convinced me to continue birding into my adult life.

Reading them again, I am struck first by the many discomforts we went through to see birds: we certainly suffered for our pleasures back in the 1970s. But they also evoke a time of innocence, when life was really much simpler: we wanted to see birds, so we got on our bikes and looked for them. In doing so we went to wonderful places and met some extraordinary people; and this combination of birds, places and people is, in essence, what birding is all about.

Funny black ducks

JANUARY 1996

I can't remember a time when I wasn't interested in birds. Big birds, small birds, brightly coloured birds in nature films, little brown birds hopping about the garden. Sparrows and swifts, gulls and geese, waders and warblers – and funny black ducks.

Yes, funny black ducks. Well, it had to start somewhere. And in my case, a lifetime's fascination with birds began with an experience I share with every child, past and present: feeding the ducks.

It was one of those dull, grey winter weekends back in 1963. Bored at home, I persuaded my mother to drive the mile or so down to the Thames at Laleham, in our yellow Ford Anglia. When we arrived, I began the ritual of chucking one piece of bread at the assembled Mallards while stuffing another in my mouth. Suddenly I stopped, my hunger overcome by a three-year-old's curiosity. I turned to my mother and asked the question: 'What are those funny black ducks?'

Despite having spent part of her childhood evacuated to the Devon countryside, my mother was not the greatest bird identification expert. In fact she had no idea what they were and tried to fob me off by changing the subject. With all the tenacity of a curious child, I persisted. And to her great credit, instead of shutting me up with another piece of bread, she promised to find out.

When we got home, she remembered that the previous Christmas one of my aunts or uncles had given me a small brown book: the *Observer's Book of Birds*. Glancing through its pages, she found the answer to the mystery: they weren't 'funny black ducks' at all, but Coots.

I picked up the book and, as they say, couldn't put it down. To my three-year-old brain, the tiny watercolour plates and abbreviated text were the fuel for a new obsession. I began to memorise the names of every single bird, starting with Magpie on page 18, and continuing until the final entry on page 217, a rather disappointing black-and-white illustration of a Capercaillie.

Many years later, having children of my own, I can appreciate the single-minded way in which I immersed myself in my new-found interest. OK, so birds didn't have to compete against Nintendo, *Jurassic Park* and the Simpsons. But watching my own five-year-old son, James, engrossed in the modern equivalent of the Observer's books, I'm glad to see that some things don't change.

I think what really captured my imagination was realising that birds were actually living, breathing creatures – not just stuck inside the pages of my little brown book. Since then, birds have become a lifetime's interest – occasionally bordering on an obsession. I can't help it. It's a bit like being a West Ham supporter – I'm stuck with it until death do us part.

Of course I'm not alone. There are millions of people around the world who enjoy watching birds, and whether their interest began at the age of three or seventy-three, they all have a story to tell about what started them off.

As to *why* we enjoy watching birds, well that's a tough one. It can't be because we enjoy being the butt of predictable jokes, or getting our feet wet, or walking for miles in the freezing cold. We do it in our spare time, yet calling it a hobby seems less than adequate. Perhaps the late James Fisher, writer and ornithologist, summed it up best when he wrote: 'The observation of birds may be a superstition, a tradition, an art, a science, a pleasure, a hobby or a bore: this depends entirely on the nature of the observer.' For me birdwatching is all of these things, and much, much more.

Down the pits

 MARCH 1996

During the years following the Second World War, strange blue holes began to appear on the Ordnance Survey map of west London. They weren't the work of aliens, the Ministry of Defence or a slapdash cartographer – but gravel-pits.

Originally dug to extract gravel for the postwar housing boom, they soon began to fill up with water, and trees and bushes started to appear. By the time I was growing up in the area during the 1960s, the 'pits', as we called them, had become a huge, outdoor playground. For an eight-year-old boy, they held an infinite promise of adventure.

I first visited Shepperton Gravel Pits in 1968. I was on a nature trail with class 2H, Saxon School, under the watchful eye of Mrs Threlfall. As we wandered in a loose crocodile along the footpath, I caught sight of my very first Great Crested Grebe – a really special bird.

After that first visit, you couldn't keep me away. In those far-off days, before the current hysteria about the danger from child molesters, youngsters were allowed to spend weekends and school holidays exploring places like this on their own. So our 'gang' – Alan, Glyn, Ian, Rob and I – spent hours on end building rafts, playing hide-and-seek and catching tadpoles in the nearby brook.

But gradually, I spent less time playing, and more time on my own, seeking out the birdlife. The Great Crested Grebes were still the main attraction, carrying their humbug-striped young on their backs like yuppie parents on a trip to IKEA. In winter, there were flocks of

Tufted Ducks and Pochard, and a small group of Cormorants; in summer, 'little brown jobs' that I finally identified as Reed Warblers.

One August Bank Holiday my mother and I went to collect elder-berries to make home-made wine – and I remember seeing two Black Terns that had dropped in during their southbound migration, dipping into the water for food.

But the most memorable event took place a year or so earlier, on 3 May 1970. My field notebook, covered with scribbled hieroglyphics, records the weather as 'blooming hot' – a daring profanity for one so young. That day, I went for a walk with Roger Trent, a tiny lad in the same class as me who had also become interested in birdwatching. We were looking out over the water and probably thinking about going off to play football, when a huge bird flew overhead.

Now normally, huge birds in south-east England are herons, but we'd seen herons and knew it couldn't be one of those. So for the rest of the day we followed the bird up and down, as it flapped lazily from one side of the pit to the other. We were pretty sure that it was some kind of bird of prey, and finally decided it must be a Buzzard. By then we were hot, grubby and tired, so we went back home for a glass of orange squash and *Thunderbirds* on the telly.

It wasn't until 14 years later, when I finally saw a migrating Osprey near the very same gravel-pits, that I realised the identity of our mystery bird. The date, the weather, the habitat and the memory of the bird itself make me sure that what we saw was one of these majestic raptors, making its return journey from Africa to Scotland.

Now, of course, it's too late to go back and find out. Soon after-wards, Roger and his family took advantage of the famous £10 a head passage and emigrated to Australia. As all ten-year-old friends do, we promised faithfully to write, but after exchanging a postcard each, the correspondence ground to a halt. Even so, more than 25 years later, I just have to open up my faded notebook to recall every moment of that warm spring day.

Heaven and hell

 FEBRUARY 1996

In Madrid, they have a saying about the city's weather. 'Nueve meses de invierno, tres de inferno – nine months of winter, three months of hell!' It's a long way from the Spanish capital to the outskirts of London, but this has always reminded me of Staines Reservoirs, where I did a lot of my early birdwatching during the 1970s.

Between September and May, and especially during the winter months, it was so cold you just wanted to lie down and die. First your fingers froze, then your toes, then everything else. It didn't help that you were standing on an exposed concrete causeway, surrounded by two huge basins of water, across which the wind whipped mercilessly. By contrast, during the summer months it could be unbearably hot, made worse by the vast flocks of midges which gathered along the causeway, preying on passing birdwatchers.

So why did anyone go there at all? Perhaps because of all the sites in west London, Staines Reservoirs was the place most likely to produce good birds. It needed to be – with Heathrow-bound aeroplanes shattering the peace every minute or two, you wouldn't go near the place unless you thought you were going to see something good.

I first visited the reservoirs with a group from the Young Ornithologists' Club, on 17 November 1969. I remember the date because at the time, I thought it might be my last day on Earth. This was before the days of thermal underwear and windproof coats, so my mother dressed me up in the kind of jacket you wear to the shops, adding a thin pair of gloves as an afterthought. I suppose I should consider myself lucky I wasn't in the short trousers we wore to school every day.

I can't remember seeing any birds through the tears brought on by a force six northerly gale. I do remember looking through my pair of (borrowed) binoculars at some black dots sitting on the water about five miles away, which I think may have been Pochard. Or Wigeon. Or just black dots.

I also remember 'dipping out' for the first time – failing to catch a glimpse of the Cormorant that everyone else seemed to have seen. Good practice for later birding failures, I suppose.

After the outing, we returned to the car park of the Crooked Billet, a Berni Inn on the nearby A30. We staggered inside, and downed a large Scotch (my mother) and a hot Bovril (me). As the feeling returned to my extremities, I vowed never again to return to this god-forsaken place.

Like so many resolutions, it didn't last. I have a battered field note-book which starts with an entry dated 28 December 1969. This time, I saw a few more birds: it lists a total of 17 species, though with hindsight some of these look a bit dubious. One thing hadn't changed, though: in the space provided for details of the weather, I simply wrote 'freezing and frostbitten'.

After that, you couldn't keep me away. During the mid-1970s, my friend Daniel and I visited Staines Reservoirs several hundred times, and kept ludicrously detailed lists of the birds we saw there. Our efforts paid off, at least occasionally. Highlights included summer-plumaged Black-necked Grebes, regular Little Gulls and, best of all, an invasion of what seemed like hundreds of Black Terns, in September 1974.

As the years went on, and I ventured further afield in search of birds, I visited Staines less and less. A quick hack up and down the causeway on New Year's Day in search of species to boost my 'year list', and the odd trip to see a rarity were about the limit. Perhaps it was the sense of familiarity, or the excitement of exploring other, more picturesque sites, but I just found I couldn't get excited about the place anymore. But it was great while it lasted.

We're all going on a summer holiday

 JULY 2005

As we set off on our family holiday to the south coast in July 2005, I had an unexpected flashback to the first time I visited the area, more than three decades ago. It was the summer of 1970, and at the age of ten I had just discovered the delights of birdwatching.

I was clutching my very first pair of binoculars, purchased for fourteen pounds, nineteen shillings and sixpence, and a pristine copy of the famous 'Peterson, Mountfort & Hollom' field guide. My mother and grandmother might have been looking forward to a relaxing rest on the beach, but I was determined to spend the whole fortnight in search of birds.

As soon as we arrived at the quiet little Hampshire resort of Milford-on-Sea, and had checked into our boarding house (imaginatively named 'Sea Walls'), I was badgering my mother to take me for a walk. Fortunately Milford is situated next to some of the best tidal mudflats in the county, so as the sun began to set I found myself gazing with delight at Oystercatchers, Dunlin, Redshank and Curlew – all new species to me, and the start of my continuing passion for wading birds.

Within a couple of days we had graduated to the nearby Keyhaven Marshes, which held even greater prizes, including Bar-tailed and Black-tailed Godwits, and my first Blackcap and Stonechat – both singing out in the open, conveniently allowing me to identify them with certainty.

When not playing crazy golf or ruining my teeth with toffee apples and candy floss, I spent the holiday happily adding new birds to my ever-growing 'life list'. Unfortunately having a field guide that included all the birds of continental Europe as well as Britain led to a few errors: such as the time I misidentified a small flock of Linnets on the lawn of our boarding house as Britain's first Bar-tailed Desert

Larks – a species confined to the arid deserts of North Africa and the Middle East.

We also visited the New Forest, where I correctly identified a Marsh Tit in the woods and a Grey Wagtail on one of the streams. But my favourite outing was a little further away, to Brownsea Island off the Dorset coast. We were given a guided tour of this delightful place, which seemed like a little piece of the Mediterranean in southern England.

This turned out to be even more appropriate. As we entered one of the hides overlooking a lagoon the warden gave an exclamation of surprise, for a hundred yards away, perched on a tree overhanging the water, was a snow-white apparition of a bird, glowing like none I had ever seen before. It was, of course, a Little Egret – a common enough bird nowadays, but at that time a true rarity. I later found out that the summer of 1970 saw a mini-invasion of these lovely birds, a foretaste of the permanent colonisation that occurred 20 years or so later.

No doubt this summer I shall see a few egrets, perhaps at Radipole Lake in Weymouth, or just on one of the pools along the coast. But nothing can take away the wonder of that very first sighting.

Master of Minsmere

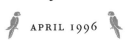

APRIL 1996

If you want to spend a spring day birdwatching anywhere in the British Isles, you'd be hard pushed to beat the RSPB's showpiece reserve at Minsmere, on the Suffolk coast. So when at the age of 13, I had the chance to visit, I couldn't wait.

It was the Easter holidays, as my mother and I headed up the A12 for the unknown reaches of East Anglia. I remember stopping off somewhere in suburban Essex – not to watch birds, but to buy my birthday present, a pair of old-fashioned Zeiss binoculars. They may look like antiques now, but these East German optics were absolutely superb, opening up a whole new world of birding experience.

I was dying to try them out and didn't have long to wait. If I remember correctly, we actually visited another RSPB reserve, Havergate Island, before making the pilgrimage to Minsmere. It was there that I saw my first Avocets.

For anyone who hasn't seen an Avocet, it is one of those birds where pictures just can't do justice to the real thing. Perched on long blue legs, with their black-and-white plumage and bizarre, upcurved bill, they look like something out of an avant-garde design competition.

I watched as one bird strolled right past our hide, utterly unconcerned at our presence. It was so close I wanted to reach out and touch it. When the RSPB adopted the Avocet as their logo they really knew what they were doing – it truly is a fabulous bird.

Next day, we finally got to Minsmere itself. I had read about it in countless books; envied those lucky enough to go there; probably even dreamt about the place. I could hardly contain my excitement.

It was a wonderful day. If my memory serves me correctly, I saw at least a dozen 'lifers' – birds I had never set eyes on before. But one still eluded us. In those days, the Marsh Harrier was on the brink of extinction as a British bird, with only a couple of breeding pairs. But it still nested on the reserve at Minsmere.

The best place to see the harriers was (and still is) the Island Mere Hide, so that's where we went. Along with a large party of loud, upper-class women, we sat in the hide and waited. Everyone scanned the reeds, but in vain. Then my mother, who didn't even have a pair of binoculars, asked no one in particular: 'What's that big bird over there?' A large man with an air of authority took a look, and in a booming voice announced: 'Well spotted Madam – it's a Marsh Harrier!'

We left the hide. Realising that this was none other than the warden, Bert Axell, I caught up with him. As youngsters do, I plied him with question after question, chattering away about the Avocets, harriers and everything else I'd seen that day. I was only dimly aware of one of the women tugging my mother's sleeve and hissing: 'This is a private party – get that child away from Mr Axell.'

Finally, after I'd exhausted my almost bottomless curiosity, Bert Axell wished me well, and we parted – he relieved, me proud and pleased to have spoken to the great man. It was only years later that I discovered that H.E. Axell, as he was better known, had a fearsome reputation. Not only had he almost single-handedly made Minsmere what it is today, but he was famous for not suffering fools gladly – even, dare I say it, for having a shortish temper. All I can say is that despite the woman's protests, he listened to me with patience, generosity and good humour.

Childhood enthusiasm is a vital commodity in all areas of knowledge – but especially in birdwatching. An unkind word or lack of encouragement, and a young person can rapidly lose interest. But when someone takes time to listen, even for just a few minutes, it rekindles the spark into what has become, for me at least, a lifelong passion.

Cordon bleu birds

MARCH 2006

When I was a young birdwatcher, there was nothing I enjoyed more than visiting new places and seeing new birds. But unlike previous generations, who had to find their own birding sites, we had a useful tool to help us. *Where to Watch Birds*, published in 1967, was the bird-finding equivalent of *The Good Food Guide*, telling us where we could enjoy five-star service and cordon bleu birds.

The author, John Gooders, had a nice line in hyperbole, describing the reserve at Cley next the Sea in north Norfolk as 'a Mecca for birdwatchers'. Even at the age of 13, I knew that this promised a feast of birds. So when Daniel and I found ourselves spending the October half-term holiday a few miles along the coast at Mundesley, we were determined to make the pilgrimage to Cley.

One of the drawbacks of *Where to Watch Birds* was that we naively treated the contents as Holy Writ, believing that we only needed to turn up to see every species mentioned in the text. This led, I recall, to some disappointing moments over the years. But not this time. For once, the book was absolutely spot-on: as we wandered around the reserve the birds were everywhere.

And what birds! A flock of Snow Buntings by the Coastguards' Café, their wings flashing white as they flew. They were accompanied by a few Lapland Buntings – a much scarcer visitor, and one that I have struggled to see since. On the marsh, a lone Whooper Swan sat regally among the lesser wildfowl, while a tiny Grey Phalarope could be seen from one of the hides. Even the beach produced new birds: including George, a Glaucous Gull. This particular individual turned up at Cley every autumn for many years, until he eventually died, to be replaced by a younger bird – named, inevitably, 'Boy George'.

On that first visit to Cley I saw no fewer than nine new species. And these were quality birds – ones that any birdwatcher, novice or not, would be pleased to see. Of course, having faithfully read our 'Bible', this was no more than we had come to expect. Yet since that first visit, despite having returned to Cley dozens of times, I have never again experienced such a wealth of unusual birds.

But the very best sighting came not at Cley, nor indeed at any other well-known site. On a rare occasion when we couldn't persuade Daniel's parents to give us a lift anywhere, we decided to take a walk inland, just to see what we could find.

We were wandering aimlessly along a footpath near the hamlet of Edingthorpe when a bird swooped out of the hedgerow and perched on a twig right in front of us. It sat like a sentinel, resplendent in its smart black, white and grey uniform. Despite never having seen one before, we immediately knew it was a Great Grey Shrike, a scarce winter visitor from Scandinavia. It sat for a few moments, then flew away, never to be seen again. But what made the experience really special was that we had found the bird ourselves, away from the classic birding sites and without the guidebook.

A gull too far

JUNE 1996

Ross's Gull is one of the world's most mysterious birds. It breeds in the remote Siberian tundra and winters in the Arctic Ocean, rarely venturing further south. Which doesn't explain what one was doing at an English south coast holiday resort back in the summer of 1974. But that's birds for you – always unpredictable.

I was on my first ever 'go-it-alone' holiday with my classmate and birding companion Daniel. In those days, despite only just having turned 14, we were allowed to get on our bikes and head vaguely in the direction of Hampshire. Loaded down with tents, primus stoves and other camping equipment, our plan was to spend a week away, discovering the ornithological delights of the New Forest.

Things went pretty well at first, and we managed to avoid the juggernauts and speed maniacs, and survived to pitch our tent. Too young to pass for 18, the local pub was out of bounds, so after cooking a meal bordering on the inedible, we retired to the tent for a night's sleep.

We spent the next two or three days in an agreeable routine of getting up, having breakfast and birdwatching until we became too tired or darkness fell, whichever came first. On the third or fourth day, we were wandering around the coastal marshes at Keyhaven, and not seeing very much, when we met a fellow birder.

'Anything about?' we enquired, in the time-honoured manner.

'Not really – except the gull, of course,' he replied.

'The gull?'

Remember, this was long before the days of rare-bird phonelines, personal pagers and all the other hi-tech aids to modern twitching. It turned out that a Ross's Gull, only the eleventh ever recorded in Britain, was still present about 20 miles along the coast, at Stanpit Marsh near Christchurch.

There was nothing else for it. We got on our bikes and went for the bird. Unfortunately, being a sunny summer Sunday, a large share of the population of southern England had also decided to visit Stanpit Marsh, which as well as being a good birding spot also boasts a beach.

We waited. And waited. And eventually gave up, and endured the 20-mile ride back to our campsite – tired, hungry and frustrated. But we weren't the sort to give up that easily. Next morning we remounted our bikes and made the long trek back to the marsh. Once again we joined the small band of eager observers perched on a sandbank.

At five past eleven, just as my stomach was beginning its usual protests, the guy sitting next to us asked quietly: 'Is this it?' We turned and looked. On the water, a hundred or so yards away, sat a small, delicate gull, its pearl-grey back contrasting with a pure white head and neck, bisected by a thin, dark line. As I focused the bins, it flew – a creature of rare grace and beauty among its commoner cousins. It was the Ross's Gull.

Twenty years later, on an unusually mild February morning, I stood with a group of twitchers by the sewage outfall at Inverness, watching another Ross's Gull. In those intervening decades, twitching has become a popular participation sport, with thousands of people racing up and down the country in search of rare birds.

I don't begrudge their enjoyment but do feel that perhaps they've taken some of the magic out of birding. I have occasional pangs of nostalgia for the days when you only heard about a rare visitor by being in the right place at the right time. And when catching up with the bird itself really meant something.

Incidentally, in our euphoria at seeing the Ross's Gull we forgot to fulfil an important promise: to phone home from time to time. When we finally returned, caked with a week's worth of dirt, our parents weren't impressed by our excuse. That's adults for you – no sense of priorities.

Half-term at Dunge . . .

 OCTOBER 1996

To many people, the phrase 'bird observatory' conjures up a picture of a purpose-built, space-age building, with an array of hi-tech optical equipment trained on the skies, ready to observe and record each passing bird.

The reality is rather different. Some observatories are in disused lighthouses, others in dilapidated shacks, held together with rusty nails and bits of rope. In terms of comfort, Dungeness Bird Observatory falls somewhere between the two, being the last in a line of old naval cottages, almost in the shadow of the nuclear power station.

I first visited Dunge, as the regulars call it, in late October 1974. At the start of the October half-term, Daniel and I rode off on the long journey from west London, he on his small-wheeled Moulton Mini, me on my five-speed Coventry Eagle. In those days, as now, the observatory provided basic accommodation for a dozen or so people, though at this late stage in the autumn only a hardy few were actually staying there.

We had an unforgettable week, although our staple diet of toast sprinkled with granulated sugar left something to be desired. Despite the late date, there were all sorts of interesting migrants, including a flock of 70 Firecrests in the area behind the observatory. We trapped a couple of these tiny, jewel-like birds, and were able to observe them at close quarters as they were ringed by the experts. We also saw a stunning Rough-legged Buzzard, an Arctic-nesting bird of prey which occasionally turns up in eastern England in autumn.

But the most memorable sighting of all occurred early one morning, when we were inside the observatory itself. The night before had brought high winds and rain, and we were lingering over our breakfast, wondering whether or not to brave the elements.

Then the door opened to reveal a man carrying what looked like a cardboard shoebox. In fact, that's exactly what it was – but inside it contained a small bundle of black-and-white feathers huddled among some newspaper. It was a Little Auk – victim of a 'wreck', during which strong winds sometimes drive these tiny sea-going birds onshore. It had been picked up somewhere along the coast and brought along to the observatory's warden, Nick Riddiford.

After nursing the bird back to consciousness and giving it food and water, the decision was taken to release it back into the wild. As two 14-year-old schoolboys, Daniel and I were flattered to be charged with this awesome responsibility.

We took the shoebox carefully down to the beach, let the bird go at the water's edge and watched as it began to float out to sea. Then, the inevitable happened. A watching Great Black-backed Gull, noticing the Little Auk's passive state, swooped down and grabbed it – and our precious cargo turned into an early lunch.

We trooped dejectedly back to the observatory to face the wrath of our colleagues. I consoled myself with the thought that the bird was obviously far too exhausted to survive, and looked forward to seeing Little Auks again in happier surroundings. Yet amazingly, I never have. Even though each autumn they pass along the east coast in their hundreds, sometimes thousands, I always arrive too early or too late.

In the last few years, thanks to better communications, Dungeness has become little more than a half-day trip from London. As a result, very few people actually stay at the observatory any more. Looking back at what we saw that week in autumn 1974, I think they're missing out.

Once Bittern

 MAY 1996

It was Mick Lane who suggested it. Mick Lane, the biggest boy in the fourth year, the captain of the rugby team, the undisputed British Bulldog champion. 'Why don't we go birdwatching?' As recollections of teenage life go, this isn't quite in the same league as 'why don't we bunk off school and go to a twenty-four-hour rave?' Then again, we didn't really go in for that sort of thing. So in the Whitsun half-term, Mick, Daniel and I packed our bags and set off for Stodmarsh, in east Kent.

It was my first real experience of birdwatching in spring, and I was, to put it bluntly, gobsmacked. Reed and Sedge Warblers were everywhere we looked. Whitethroats sang from any available perch, swaying in the breeze. And every few minutes, a Cuckoo flew past.

It's probably nostalgia that creates this rose-tinted picture of delight. But one bird will stay in my memory until I finally hang up my binoculars. A Little Bittern. Not a 'little Bittern', but a Little Bittern: the Bittern's rare and elusive southern European relative.

The day was Sunday, 25 May, and it was a scorcher. By lunchtime, my stomach was in a state of open rebellion. Daniel and Mick seemed happy to survive on the bowl of cornflakes we'd had for breakfast, but I wasn't. They put up with my whingeing for a while, and then gave in, so we walked back to the pub. Following in that great British tradition, in those days the Red Lion stopped serving food at 1.30 on a Sunday afternoon. We made do with a couple of packets of beef and onion crisps, and a lemonade. As we wandered back, we weren't in the best of moods. Then, we met a man with the look of someone with urgent news to impart.

'I've just seen a male Little Bittern,' he gasped. So did we. We'd just missed the bird of a lifetime. And it was my fault – or at least, my stomach's . . .

But the great thing about Stodmarsh is that you can only go in two directions, unless you want to get your feet wet. So we strode forward along the footpath. I was just beginning to have my doubts when I noticed a bird flying alongside, low above the reeds, with trailing legs, yellow underparts and huge, pink wing-patches.

I can't even begin to describe the feeling as I watched my first Little Bittern passing by in the afternoon sun. What a bird! It stayed another two days, during which we got another couple of fleeting views, as it briefly rose from the reeds, before plunging back out of sight.

The next afternoon our peace of mind was disturbed by a manic figure carrying a battered pair of binoculars. At first he couldn't speak, having run all the way from the car park. Fighting for breath, he managed to gasp a question: 'Did . . . Did . . . Didn't you ring anybody? Don't you know anyone on the grapevine?'

We didn't, and hadn't. We were blissfully unaware that such a shady organisation, by which news of a rare bird was spread among Britain's twitchers, even existed. There's a word for it now – suppression – one of the deadliest sins a birdwatcher can commit. But we hadn't suppressed the Little Bittern – we just hadn't got any two-pence pieces for the phone. Eventually our interrogator calmed down, and settled down to wait for the bird's appearance. But despite sleeping out overnight, he never did get to see it.

Two decades later, part of me is sad that the Little Bittern remains a very rare bird in Britain. But less charitably, I rub my hands with glee at the thought of all those twitchers who still haven't got it on their British list.

It remains one of the greatest moments in my birdwatching life, and it probably always will. Like Cup Finals and Wimbledon, ice cream and summer holidays, some things are never quite as good as when you were 15 years old . . .

Albert memorial

 JULY 1996

By the time I left Cambridge University in the summer of 1982, I'd more or less given up watching birds. Along with stamp-collecting and kicking a football about in the park, I suppose I felt it belonged with childhood pastimes and should now be left behind.

After graduating with a mediocre degree in English Literature, I felt I deserved a holiday, but everyone else was either working or broke. So I decided to give the birds one last try, and headed north to the Shetland Isles. For those of you who think that Shetland is stuck in a box somewhere off Aberdeen, let me put you straight. The island of Unst – the northernmost inhabited place in the British Isles – is as far from London as Prague, and a great deal harder to reach.

The cheapest (though certainly not the quickest) route involved taking the train to Aberdeen, followed by an overnight boat to the islands' main town of Lerwick. I chose not to pay extra for a cabin, so at 6 a.m. I awoke to a cricked neck and the sound of the ship's engine slowing down. I dragged myself up on deck to find that we were passing through a tunnel of rock, between two dark, forbidding crags. I had finally arrived.

I took the bus north, as the only passenger. For the first time I saw the beauty of Shetland: stark, windswept, treeless – and full of birding promise. Two hours later, I reached the village of Baltasound.

I don't know what I'd been expecting – perhaps an ancient croft, with Mrs McMiggins standing at the gate to welcome me with a hot toddy and an open fire. What I actually found was a three-bedroom semi, uncannily like the one I'd grown up in, but with better wind-proofing. Inside, one perfectly normal family, sitting round the gas fire (the weather can be treacherous in Shetland, even in July).

Next morning, I set off for the legendary seabird colony of Hermaness. Generally, when you visit one of Britain's best-known bird sites at the height of the season, you come across fellow birders. But for six hours I didn't meet a soul. For someone who, having been brought up in London, used to get nervous on a half-empty bus, this was seriously remote.

As I wandered across the open country, I felt a rush of air past my head. It was a Great Skua, whose breeding territory I had inadvertently entered, engaging in behaviour quaintly known as 'mobbing'. I now know that the best antidote is to raise a stick above your head to provide a focus for the skua's attack. But not having brought a stick or any other long, hard implement, I did the next best thing and ducked.

The bird swept past – close enough for me to feel a brief flurry of wings. I turned away, feeling remarkably calm. But coming towards me out of the sun was an Arctic Skua, whose streamlined shape and manoeuvrability are to its larger relative what a Phantom jet is to a Wellington bomber.

I did what any self-respecting birdwatcher would do. I ran. Fortunately I stopped before I got to the cliff edge, where I collapsed in a shuddering heap. Before I could get my breath back, I took in the awesome sight. The sky was filled with thousands and thousands of Gannets. As well as being one of the experiences of a lifetime, this also presented me with a problem. Somewhere among the wheeling throng was a unique bird: Albert, the only albatross in the northern hemisphere (Albert Ross – get it?).

I never did get to see Albert. He was supposed to be perched on the cliff-face, guarding a nesting-site in the hope that a passing Alberta would come by. Despite searching for an hour or more, I just couldn't see him and reluctantly turned for home.

The day didn't end quite as well as it had begun. I sat with the McMiggins clan, watching England play an uninspiring 0–0 draw with Spain, which put them out of the 1982 World Cup. The only comfort was that Scotland had been knocked out, as usual, in the first round. But despite missing out on the albatross, the combination of beautiful scenery, thousands of Gannets and a skua attack had fortunately convinced me that birding was something I still wanted to do.

CHAPTER 2

Spreading my wings

1983–1997

H aving decided that birdwatching was not just a passing phase, but something I wanted to do throughout my adult life, I spent much of the 1980s drifting aimlessly around Britain in search of new birds to add to my 'British List'.

Looking back, it is hard to recall just how insular and parochial the pastime of watching birds was in those days. Birdwatchers (not yet transformed into 'birders') were either solitary individuals or went around in tight cliques, rebuffing any approach from an outsider. My lack of nostalgic reminiscences from that decade reflects my sense of isolation and also that my new job as a television producer with the BBC and a young family were taking up much of my time.

I don't miss the 1980s, but as the 1990s got under way things took a turn for the better. On a rare foreign trip to Israel in 1989 I met an amiable chap called Neil, who lived a few miles around the M25 from me. As often happens, we swapped addresses but never quite got around to getting in touch. Coincidentally, the following year we bumped into each other on a seabird-watching trip out of Penzance, and decided to team up. Since then we have enjoyed many memorable birding experiences together and have become great friends.

Another piece of the jigsaw fell into place in 1995 when, after more than a decade trying, I finally persuaded the BBC to commission a series on birdwatching, with me as the producer. *Birding with Bill Oddie* was not only a critical and ratings success, it also changed my life. From then on, my lifetime's passion was also my job, and although I initially had some misgivings about these two areas of my life converging, I was proved wrong.

Working with Bill for the past decade has been a privilege and a pleasure. As this and subsequent chapters reveal, we have been fortunate to travel all over Britain – and indeed much of the world – in search of birds. To paraphrase a recent advertising campaign: 'If Carlsberg made jobs, mine would probably be the best in the world.'

Petrel puzzler

 SEPTEMBER 1996

We've all had the frustrating experience of a brief glimpse of 'something different' – a bird that looks unusual, but which you don't see well enough to identify. Generally it's best just to put the episode down to experience. But once or twice in a lifetime, a birder may experience the ultimate frustration: seeing a bird that you *know* is something good, but whose identity you just can't pin down.

My own 'one that got away' happened back in September 1983. I fancied a few days off work, so I drove my battered Ford Cortina up to north Norfolk. The next morning, my companion and I wandered along to the beach at Cley, which as every birdwatcher knows, can be a great place for passing seabirds. However, mid-morning on a bright, clear, windless day is hardly likely to produce an avalanche of unusual sightings.

So it proved. Despite watching for an hour or so, we didn't see much more than a few of the local gulls flapping along the tideline. Apart, that is, from the petrel. We'd only just got ourselves comfortable on the shingle, next to two or three other optimists, when I caught sight of a small, dark bird 'shearing' over the waves just beyond the tideline. I was about to yell 'shearwater' when someone else called 'Leach's Petrel – flying left!'

We watched for a minute or two, until the bird was out of range. Then we looked at each other in delight and congratulated ourselves on our good fortune. We were so elated that I committed the birder's cardinal sin: I failed to take any field notes. After all, we had all agreed it was a Leach's – and for me it was a new bird as well!

It was only when I got home, and leafed through a few field guides, that I began to have my doubts. According to the experts, Leach's Petrel is supposed to have a dancing, tern-like flight, a pronounced kink in the wing, a forked tail and an indistinct, V-shaped rump. The bird I'd seen had none of these characteristics, at least as far as I could recall. So I assumed it must be a Storm Petrel, with a typical all-dark plumage and plain white rump.

Two problems. First, Storm Petrels are a very rare sight off the north Norfolk coast, almost always being sighted in poor weather, when they are driven close inshore. Second, I have seen numerous Storm Petrels since, and though their plumage fits my mystery bird, their 'jizz' (or general appearance) certainly doesn't.

Every Stormie I've watched has a weak, fluttering flight, more like a bat than a bird. In contrast, the flight of the Norfolk petrel was strong and direct, on long, straight wings. So what was it? A Leach's, which somehow managed to conceal all its distinctive field marks? Or a Storm, flying differently from normal owing to the unusually calm conditions?

Or could it have been something else? That straight-winged look, that broad, white rump, that shearwater-like flight – they all point to the rare Wilson's Petrel, straying round the coast from its usual haunts out in the Atlantic.

Of course, now I will never know. A few years later my companion on that day died, tragically, from heatstroke while birding in Australia. The other observers? Who knows – but if you're reading this, and you've got a dodgy Leach's Petrel on your list, do get in touch!

The moral of this sorry tale? Never assume. Never go along with the crowd if you have a shred of doubt. And always, always take detailed field notes. You can use a notebook, tape-recorder, palmtop computer or back of an old envelope – it doesn't matter. Just do it, or, like me, you will live to regret 'the one that got away'.

The Scilly season

 OCTOBER 1995

Few birdwatchers lucky enough to be on the Isles of Scilly in mid-October 1985 are ever likely to forget the experience. It was one of those rare autumns during which the birds appeared to come from all points of the compass to make landfall on these delightful islands off the south-west of the British Isles.

I arrived by helicopter from Penzance, weighed down with the weatherproof clothing I'd worn to combat the worst of the British weather. As I disembarked, I was met by an extraordinary scene: a crowd of birdwatchers, most in shirt-sleeves, staring intently at what appeared to be a small patch of scrubby grass.

It *was* a small patch of scrubby grass, but being on the Isles of Scilly in autumn, it concealed a rare bird. This was a Bobolink, a North American species which looks like an anorexic Corn Bunting. This was just one of several American vagrants which had managed to cross the Atlantic Ocean during the westerly gales of the week before.

Getting a good view of the Bobolink meant I had missed the bus to the islands' capital, Hugh Town, so I shouldered my rucksack and began the long but pleasant walk. I soon realised that a thick jumper and waterproofs were a mistake. The sun shone high in the sky, and temperatures were up in the seventies – great weather for tourists, but not so likely to produce a crop of rare birds.

Or so I thought. In fact, October 1985 proved to be the best ever for rare vagrants on Scilly, with birds turning up from west, south and east. As well as the obliging Bobolink, there were up to 15 American land-birds of six species on the islands. These included both Yellow-billed and Black-billed Cuckoos – the latter posing exhausted on the lower branches of a tree for a crowd of almost a thousand contented birders, in full view of a hungry-looking cat. The next day, the cuckoo was nowhere to be seen.

Transatlantic vagrants are more or less annual on Scilly, though their numbers vary from year to year depending on the timing and intensity of westerly gales. More unusual was a crop of visitors from southern Europe, presumably due to the spell of light southerly winds that had brought such good weather to the islands. These Mediterranean wanderers included a stunning Bee-eater, which posed for all-comers on the island of Tresco.

As if this wasn't enough, in mid-October birds started to arrive from the east, too. Yellow-browed Warblers, an annual visitor from Siberia, seemed to be everywhere, and on the 15th a Booted Warbler was discovered in a clump of bushes on Penninis Head, St Mary's. These birds had travelled thousands of miles in the wrong direction across Asia and Europe, due to a combination of bad navigation and the right weather conditions. Where they went after leaving the islands, nobody knows.

Café society – Norfolk-style

 SEPTEMBER 1995

It's not far from the truth to say that good weather for birdwatchers is bad weather for everyone else. To put it another way, wind and rain often bring the most interesting birds to our shores – especially in autumn, when migrants on their first journey may go astray during bad weather. But it doesn't always have to be like that. Once in a while, glorious autumn sunshine and soaring temperatures can be accompanied by fantastic birds.

Back in late September 1986 I planned a trip to East Anglia with a couple of friends – both relatively novice birdwatchers. As we set out from London I looked at the clear blue sky and reflected that even if we didn't see any birds, at least we'd get a decent suntan. I was right about the weather, which stayed warm and sunny throughout. Fortunately, I was wrong about the birds.

We started off at the RSPB's best-known reserve – Minsmere, in east Suffolk. There, we came across the first rarity of the trip: a juvenile Red-backed Shrike, perched on bushes near the sluice. We also saw an unseasonal Red-necked Grebe, moulting out of its gaudy breeding plumage.

Heading round the coast towards north Norfolk, we stopped off at Cley Marshes. A quick seawatch produced a variety of commoner seabirds, including passing Gannets, Red-throated Divers and a very obliging Arctic Skua. This bird lived up to its piratical reputation, chasing terns up and down the beach in order to persuade them to regurgitate their food.

After an enjoyable and productive morning, we headed towards the legendary Nancy's Café for lunch. This establishment, alas now closed, was located in the back parlour of a tiny terraced cottage in the middle of Cley. For a few years, before the advent of hi-tech bird information services, this humble eatery was the centre of the twitchers' 'grapevine'.

People phoned Nancy's from all over the country, leaving messages about rare bird sightings, or more often, wanting to find the latest 'gen' on what had been seen elsewhere.

This made the uninterrupted consumption of food well-nigh impossible. No sooner had you lifted a forkful of baked beans to your mouth, than you had to answer the phone to yet another anxious caller, demanding to know if the latest rarity was still present on Scilly or Fair Isle.

As we approached Nancy's, smacking our lips at the thought of our well-deserved meal, another birdwatcher ran out. His rather flustered appearance suggested that he might be in a hurry. Sure enough, as he passed us, he blurted out the words: 'Citrine Wagtail. Just been found. Blakeney Harbour.'

His rapid departure presented us with a dilemma. Did we forgo the prospect of lunch, leap in the car and follow him to see this rare and unexpected Siberian vagrant? Or did we stick to our original itinerary?

It was a foregone conclusion, really. So it was not until an hour or so later, fortified by poached eggs and copious cups of tea, that the three of us wandered up to the small crowd of people by the harbour at Blakeney. There, we asked the usual question, heard at every twitchers' gathering. 'Still showing?'

It was, and we enjoyed excellent, close-up views of the wagtail, the first ever seen in Norfolk. OK, so it didn't look all that different from our familiar Pied Wagtail, but it was a humbling experience watching a bird that had flown thousands of miles off course, impelled by some mysterious form of wanderlust.

Nevertheless, I must confess to a certain satisfaction that, unlike the other observers there, we had the satisfaction of a full stomach. After all, as even the most dedicated twitcher must accept, man cannot live by birds alone.

Dream birds

 NOVEMBER 1996

When you start birdwatching, there are some birds you always dream of seeing. But when you do finally manage to find them, it can sometimes be a bit of a disappointment. Once in a while, though, your dream bird is as wonderful in real life as you hoped and imagined.

The Waxwing has always had an air of mystery about it. Waxwings are birds of the far north, breeding in the pine forests of Scandinavia and Siberia. In autumn, they become nomadic: roaming far and wide in search of their favourite food, berries. But if the berry crop fails in northern Europe, Waxwings head south and west, in what ornithologists call an irruption. Most years, only a few Waxwings are recorded in the British Isles, but in a good year, there may be thousands.

When they do turn up, they can often be surprisingly easy to see. Their berry diet means that they frequently visit gardens, where they usually stay until they have stripped a bush bare, before moving on in search of the next free lunch. The 1970s, the period when I began serious birding, wasn't a very good decade for Waxwings. There were one or two minor invasions during the 1980s, but I still never managed to catch up with them. Then, in autumn 1988, the birders' grapevine buzzed with welcome news: large flocks of Waxwings had been sighted up and down Britain's east coast. An irruption year was under way.

One dull day in November, I had to visit Norwich on business. The meeting dragged on and on, and I didn't get away until mid-afternoon. But instead of taking the A11 back to London, I headed east, to the little village of Sutton.

Like several Norfolk villages, Sutton has a small pond as its centrepiece. According to the telephone information service Birdline East Anglia, a flock of about 30 Waxwings was supposed to be regularly visiting the trees around the pond. I parked my car alongside, got out and waited. And waited. There was still no sign of my quarry, though there were several false alarms: a group of Starlings; the usual resident sparrows. I was beginning to feel a little out of place, as curtains began to twitch, and passing villagers gave me suspicious looks.

As dusk approached, I was just thinking about giving up. Then, at last, my faith was rewarded. A flock of birds flew up into the branches above my head. Surely they weren't yet another bunch of Starlings? I tentatively raised my binoculars to my eyes and gasped at the vision of beauty before me. A small, plump bird, with a plumage of a colour so subtle that I can hardly begin to describe it. Basically brown, yes, but with hints and tints of pink, ochre and sepia; black wingtips edged with yellow and red; and the delicate wispy crest above a black highwayman's mask.

I watched in quiet delight as the birds began to gorge themselves on bright red berries, then launched themselves into the late afternoon air, flycatching for passing insects. A few minutes later, guided by some unseen signal, they took off and flew away. I wanted to shout out loud, knock on doors, accost passers-by – have you seen them? Aren't they beautiful? Don't you realise what fantastic visitors you have?! But being British, I simply got back into the car and drove off to have a quiet, celebratory drink in a country pub.

All at sea

 AUGUST 1993

Most birdwatchers are landlubbers at heart. But for one special breed of enthusiast, the call of the sea is just too strong to resist. 'Seawatchers', as they are known, often do just that. They spend their time on a windswept coastal headland, gazing out to sea, waiting for seabirds to pass by. It can be a lonely and frustrating pastime: truly oceanic species such as petrels and shearwaters rarely come near land, and when they do, views are often distant and brief.

Fortunately for the sanity of seawatchers, help is at hand. Sometime during the 1980s, the penny dropped. Rather than sitting on some god-forsaken cliff, waiting for the birds to come to you, why not go to the birds themselves? This insight resulted in the first of many pelagic trips, in which the birdwatchers charter a boat and sail far out to sea to discover these ocean-going birds on their home ground.

I went on my first pelagic trip in August 1990, sailing at dawn from Penzance on the passenger ship *Scillonian*, with 300 keen birders aboard. Our destination was the Western Approaches, out in the Atlantic some hundred miles or so beyond the Isles of Scilly. Our aim was to do what the seabirds do, and follow the fishing boats. By listening on a shortwave radio, we soon tracked down a fleet of small craft from the Spanish port of Bilbao.

Seabirds have an extraordinary sense of smell, which enables them to locate a source of food from several miles away. When we approached the fishing boats the sea was virtually devoid of birds, apart from the usual flocks of gulls. But, as the trawler's crew threw the gutted fish-offal overboard, the birds began to appear over the horizon as if attracted by some invisible signal.

The first arrivals were yet more gulls, accompanied by a skua or two. Then, straining our eyes, we saw a flicker of tiny wings in the far distance, signalling the approach of the first Storm Petrels. These minuscule birds, hardly bigger than a House Martin, have a superficially similar appearance, with a black body and conspicuous white rump. They feed on fluttering wings, plunging down to pick morsels of food off the surface of the water.

Seasoned pelagic voyagers have dispensed with the need to find a fishing fleet, by following the 'bring-your-own' philosophy. They spend the night before a trip visiting the local fish-quay, collecting up any remains they can find. They place their 'catch' in barrels, and add popcorn or Rice Krispies, to provide an added visual stimulus for passing seabirds. The resulting ghastly concoction is called 'chum', and the action of spreading it on the water is known as 'chumming'.

Chumming requires a strong stomach, though fortunately on this trip we enjoyed perfect sunny weather, with hardly a breeze to ruffle the waves. Our final tally included six Sabine's Gulls, a high Arctic species en route to spending the winter in Africa; several magnificent Great Shearwaters, cruising low over the water like a pod of airborne sharks; and even a bogus 'albatross' – which turned out to be a young Gannet. We returned to port late in the evening, sunburnt yet satisfied.

The interesting thing about pelagic trips is their sheer unpredictability. One time you may see thousands of birds, the next you can draw a complete blank. But a pelagic always gives you a unique insight into the lives of some of our most mysterious birds.

Big day in the suburbs

JANUARY 1994

If you were planning a winter day's birdwatching, the outskirts of west London might not seem the best place to start. Surely the Norfolk marshes, Solway Firth or one of the south coast estuaries would be more productive? Perhaps. Yet it is quite possible to see as many as 70 different species in a single day in the London suburbs, even with a New Year hangover to contend with. For the past few years, my birding companion Neil and I have shrugged off the excesses of New Year's Eve and, along with thousands of other birdwatchers throughout Britain, spent 1 January out in the field.

In fact this year we cheated, waiting until 2 January. By first light (around 8am) we were ticking off some familiar birds on Neil's birdtable. Ten minutes later, we discovered local specialities Grey Wagtail and Green Sandpiper in nearby Cassiobury Park. Just a mile or so from Watford town centre, this damp, wooded park plays host to a fine selection of woodland birds, including Siskins, Treecreepers and two species of woodpecker.

Leaving the park, we travelled along the M25 to Virginia Water. A quick search failed to produce the expected Mandarin Duck, but during a walk around Wraysbury Gravel Pits we got good views of a pair of wintering Smew, the males looking as if they had been pieced together from a precious vase that someone had dropped and tried to repair. These lakes, close to Heathrow Airport, are one of the main British haunts of this attractive duck. As we watched, Concorde passed low overhead, momentarily shattering the peace.

By noon we had amassed a total of 50 species. It's from now on that the going gets tough, with each new species a bonus. One year we took until early afternoon to see House Sparrows, and even common wintering birds such as Redwings and Fieldfares can be surprisingly elusive.

This year, Staines Moor was too flooded for waders, but the vast basins of Staines Reservoirs brought a surprise. They'd been drained: bad news for the duck, but good for us. Despite the distance from the coast, they provided refuge for six species of wader: thousands of Lapwings, a hundred or so Dunlin, and a few Redshank, Ruffs, Golden Plovers and Snipe.

Another walk around Wraysbury, and we flushed a pair of Kingfishers, one fleeing along a muddy path – a brilliant flash of blue and orange in the late afternoon light. We've seen Kingfishers at different places four years in a row, but it's still one of the day's highlights.

Finally, with less than an hour's daylight remaining, we headed for Magna Carta Lane, Wraysbury. There, amidst a quintessentially English scene of fields and hedges, we caught up with three 'alien' species. A cock Pheasant, whose ancestors were brought here by the Romans, strutted along a field edge. A Little Owl, originally introduced in the Victorian era, squealed in the dusk. And most extraordinary of all, as we gazed across the Thames to the site of the signing of the Magna Carta, a high-pitched series of shrieks pierced the sky: a flock of six bright green birds, more streamlined than any native British species. They were Ring-necked Parakeets, going to roost on an island in the Thames at Runnymede.

Among birdwatchers, this bird divides opinion. Some detest them, believing that, like the Canada Goose and Ruddy Duck, they will eventually overrun our native avifauna. Others thrill to the sight of wild parakeets adding a splash of colour to the drab winter scene. As dusk fell, Neil and I agreed that we fall firmly into the latter camp, and that the Ring-necked Parakeet has a deserved place among the 71 species on our Big Day list.

150 not out

 MAY 1994

Friday, 13 May might not be the best day to rush around chasing birds, but that didn't put us off. We were taking part in a charity bird race, run by BirdLife International. The idea was to raise sponsorship cash for Project Halmahera in Indonesia, while undergoing an endurance test that would put the SAS to shame.

The rules are simple. You have 24 hours in which to see (or hear) as many species of bird as possible, in a single county. We chose Norfolk, which generally produces the highest total, and where the British record of 159 species was set in May 1992. Our aim was more modest – to reach 150 species if possible.

At 2.48 a.m. we chalked up bird number one – a cacophony of Nightingales, singing their hearts out on Salthouse Heath. We didn't actually *see* them, as it was pitch-dark, and stayed that way for the following couple of hours. But this didn't stop my sharp-eared colleagues Sacha, Jo and team-leader Mark from totting up more than 20 species by first light, on song and call alone.

Mark is the local expert, so we followed his directions inland, towards a dawn chorus in the Norfolk Brecks. On the way, we added Tawny Owl (on a roadside post) and a ghostly Barn Owl, dazzled by our headlights as it floated across the road. Before dawn we were at

Lynford Arboretum, one of the few large mixed woodlands in Norfolk. We found the usual range of songbirds, along with a couple of unexpected species such as a Golden Pheasant croaking in the undergrowth. For the rest of the day we followed a long and winding route around the county, dropping in on known sites for hard-to-see species, and famous hotspots like the RSPB reserve at Titchwell.

The key to a successful bird race is the weather. Beforehand, it should be bad enough to blow in some interesting birds. But on the day itself, wind and rain drive birds under cover and make the bird-racers themselves thoroughly miserable. We were fortunate. A run of easterly winds had deposited a selection of unusual visitors, while to our relief, the weather on the 13th was sunny and warm.

The day's highlight came at an unlikely spot – a road junction in the village of Narborough. A flock of Jackdaws flying overhead, with one larger bird, caught our eye. Binoculars revealed an unfortunate Osprey being mobbed by its smaller companions. This may have been one of the Scottish Ospreys, but was perhaps more likely to have drifted off course while on the way from its African winter-quarters to Scandinavia. Either way, it had the desired effect of providing a surge of much-needed adrenaline.

In contrast, some quite familiar species can be hard to find. Kingfishers are scarce in Norfolk, and predictably, we failed to see one. We also missed out on migrant songbirds, which were very thin on the ground. However, during the course of the day we did tot up 13 species of duck, 29 different waders and 9 warblers.

As darkness fell, we had managed to log 148 species, frustratingly short of our target. Fortunately, Mark's local knowledge paid off, when we came across a Little Owl in the grounds of a stately home. Then it was back to where we started, the Norfolk Naturalists' Trust reserve at Cley. A quick stagger across a darkened marsh, and we heard the distant but unmistakable sound of a booming Bittern. We'd reached 150, and it was time to adjourn to the George for a well-earned pint.

Belfast birds

 JUNE 1994

The words Belfast and birdwatching don't often get mentioned in the same breath. Yet last month, on a hill overlooking the city, I watched the aerial acrobatics of a pair of Peregrine Falcons. I caught sight of the first bird as I reached the top of a steep slope, above a sheer cliff-face. It was holding something in its talons – probably one of the ubiquitous Meadow Pipits that breed on the grassy moors and are the Peregrine's staple diet during the breeding season. As it called its shrill, repetitive call, it was joined by the second bird, a smaller male. The two twisted and turned on stiff, powerful wings in the updraughts by the cliff.

We sat on the summit, caught our breath, and enjoyed the view, while the falcons performed their gymnastic display against an incongruous urban backdrop. From this side view they looked like fighter jets, cruising effortlessly through the air, and changing speed with the barest flicker of a wing.

When hunting, Peregrines tower high into the clouds, then fold back their wings before plunging headlong towards their oblivious prey. This spectacle is known as a 'stoop', during which the bird may reach speeds of 180mph. The Belfast birds seemed content to ride the air-currents – perhaps they just weren't hungry . . .

The Peregrine is one of conservation's rare success stories. In the last two or three decades it has truly come back from the brink – after a double whammy threatened to wipe out the British and Irish populations. Before the Second World War Peregrines were fairly common throughout the northern and western parts of the British Isles, especially on high ground and near coasts. But when war broke out, the falcon fell victim to a systematic campaign waged by the Ministry of Defence, who believed Peregrines were killing thousands of homing pigeons used to carry vital messages. More than 600 pairs – a third of the prewar population – were shot, and the bird was eradicated from many of its former haunts.

Then, just as the species was beginning to recover from one disaster, a second struck. During the late 1950s, it was discovered that Peregrine egg-shells had become far thinner and more prone to breakage than before. Numbers began to drop dramatically, and it seemed the species might finally disappear from the British Isles. But after some brilliant detective work by scientists at the Nature Conservancy, the culprit was discovered. Organochlorine pesticides such as DDT were entering the food chain and accumulating in lethal levels in the Peregrine, via its prey. After a campaign by conservation organisations, these pesticides were banned, and the recovery began.

Since the 1960s, the Peregrine population has risen steadily, with a recent survey estimating almost 1500 breeding pairs. Though still in danger from unscrupulous falconers and egg-collectors, the species has now begun to recolonise its former haunts. Sometimes, in autumn and winter, it can be seen at coastal marshes, where it preys on waders and wildfowl. But for me, it's hard to beat that sight of a pair of Peregrines in their mastery of the steel-grey skies above the Belfast skyline.

Purple patch

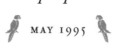 MAY 1995

I used to live in north London, about as far from the English countryside as you can get. I only knew summer had come when I heard the sounds of screaming as I walked to the tube station. Not the agonies of the city commuter, but the cries of a bird – the Swift, one of the latest summer visitors to return to Europe. They arrive in southern England in late April or early May, and in northern counties a week or two later. With their cigar-shaped bodies and scythe-like wings, they are one of the most typical sights – and sounds – of summer in the city.

This year, despite the fine weather at the end of April, the Swifts didn't appear – at least not in my little corner of suburbia. May Day came and went, still with no sign of their return. Impatient to see them, I headed to the RSPB's reserve at Minsmere in Suffolk.

The weather could hardly have been better – for the birds, at least. I soon caught up with the Swifts, screaming across the blue skies above the village of Westleton. Unfortunately the same cloudless skies had encouraged many migrating waders to press on north to their Arctic breeding grounds, rather than stopping off to refuel on Minsmere's lush lagoons.

In compensation, various warblers were proclaiming their new-found territories with song. Every bush, it seemed, contained an acrobatic Whitethroat; every reedbed a Sedge Warbler; every patch of trees a Chiffchaff, Willow Warbler or Blackcap. Even the picnic area by the car park played host to a Garden Warbler, belting out its rapid burst of song.

But the sovereign of songsters was more elusive. Half-way round the reserve I finally heard the unmistakable sound of the Nightingale, pouring a medley of rich, mellow notes into the morning air. While I waited for the bird to emerge from the dense thicket, I could hear the most famous summer sound of all – the call of the Cuckoo.

Minsmere is best-known for three rare breeding species. Its greatest success, and the emblem of the RSPB itself, is the famous Avocet. A hundred or so pairs of this elegant wader nest on the 'scrape', the lagoons and islands in the centre of the reserve. I watched as they waded waist-deep in the brackish water, dipping in their long, upturned bills to catch their tiny prey. From another hide, I enjoyed the spectacle of Marsh Harriers, quartering the reeds on their long, broad wings. Occasionally the male would rise high in the air, then plummet down to pass food to his mate.

Minsmere's third speciality, the Bittern, was once widespread in East Anglia, but the draining of the fens confined it to a handful of sites. Bitterns are normally so elusive that you doubt their very existence, but this day was a welcome exception. Perhaps encouraged by the warm weather, they emerged from the reeds: two in flight, and one feeding right in front of the hide.

The icing on the cake was a sighting of an even rarer bird. Returning from Africa, a Purple Heron had overshot its intended destination and had been carried across the sea to Minsmere by light, southerly winds. After a long wait, I was rewarded when it flew up and perched momentarily on a tree, showing its deep, purple plumage and serpent-like neck. Minutes later, it flew back into the reeds, never to be seen again.

And when I finally got back to the London suburbs, there were the Swifts, screaming across the skies above my head as if they'd never been away.

Back at Minsmere

 MAY 2006

Ten years ago this month, I found myself braving bitter winds on a grey day at the RSPB's Minsmere reserve in Suffolk. Not particularly good weather for birding, and even worse for filming. For we were attempting to make the very first episode of the television series *Birding with Bill Oddie*, and the weather was against us.

Despite this inauspicious start, things did hot up, in terms both of weather and birds. By the end of the three-day shoot we had assembled a series of sequences which fulfilled our ambition of conveying what birding is really like to a mass television audience, most of whom had never even picked up a pair of binoculars.

We began the programme with a dawn chorus, which in early May meant leaving our hotel at 3 a.m., in order to be in place when the first bird sang. Fortunately there was a full moon, which added to the aesthetics of the scene, and that morning the gods were kind to us, and the chilly wind dropped to a light breeze. As the sun came up, we trudged back to Minsmere's newly opened tearooms for breakfast, knowing that we had captured something really special.

From then on, fuelled by a combination of adrenaline and a fry-up, we just kept going. Breakfast itself was interrupted when Bill caught sight of the Sand Martin colony in the reserve's old car park; after which we followed the time-honoured route around the 'Scrape', a lagoon surrounded by strategically placed hides.

We soon realised that Bill had a natural ability to respond brilliantly to whatever he saw – or in the case of singing Reed and Sedge Warblers, didn't see. These elusive songbirds stayed hidden in the reeds, prompting him to perform a memorable monologue on how to separate the two species by their song.

After a spot of seawatching, we headed back into the woods, which are usually rather quiet at this time of day. But we had reckoned without the birds' ability to surprise us. Coming across a little huddle of people staring up into the trees, we posed the obvious question: 'Anything about?' There was: four baby Tawny Owls, looking like giant feather dusters. Despite our combined total of more than 80 years birding between us, neither Bill nor I had ever seen such a sight before.

Fortified by this unexpected encounter, we paid a visit to the Island Mere Hide. Apparently growing out of the surrounding reeds, this high-rise structure gives excellent views over the surrounding lagoons. When I first visited Minsmere, back in 1973, the three Marsh Harriers I saw from this hide represented the entire British breeding population. Thanks to the conservation work of the RSPB, the harriers are now doing very well, but it is always a thrill to see them. They performed beautifully for the cameras, the male chasing the female low over the water in a display flight.

The day and the programme were rounded off by a real bonus: four Common Cranes coming into roost as the sun set. And although I have made dozens of programmes with Bill Oddie, that first episode will always be my favourite.

A wild goose chase

 FEBRUARY 1997

There are an awful lot of geese on Islay – around 45,000 of them, in fact. They spend most of the day eating grass, munching away like contented cows. Occasionally they stop for a moment or two, to bathe, defecate or fly around a little. Then they start eating grass again. Finally, as dusk begins to fall, they take to the skies in a flurry of wings, before going to roost, falling to earth like a team of drunken parachutists.

Two-thirds of Islay's geese – around 30,000 birds – are Barnacles, with almost all the remainder being Greenland Whitefronts. This represents a substantial proportion of the world population for both species, making Islay one of the most important bird sites in north-west Europe.

According to legend, Barnacle Geese are so-called because they are supposed to hatch from tiny shellfish. Perhaps whoever thought that one up had been sipping a little too much of the local water – after it had been turned into Lagavulin, Laphroaig, or another of the many kinds of malt whisky made on the island. This gets its celebrated taste – and golden-brown colour – from the peat in the island's streams. Indeed the whole place is bathed in a golden-brown light from a sun which barely manages to drag itself above the horizon, even at midday. It's the kind of light TV producers pray for, as it makes every shot look as if it were painted by Rembrandt.

Because of the short amount of daylight during midwinter, Islay's birds form flocks around every available source of food. We came across vast groups of Rooks and Jackdaws, with smaller numbers of Ravens, Hooded Crows and the rare and comical Chough. Best of all, in the dunes below Ardnave Point, we stumbled upon a tight little flock of Snow Buntings. These lived up to their name by swirling around in the sky like animated snowflakes, before returning to earth, where they continued to feed.

Islay is also the home of a population of genuine, wild Rock Doves – ancestors of the much-reviled Feral Pigeon. In contrast to our familiar city birds, they are very wary, and when we emerged from the car we were using as a mobile hide, they flew away immediately.

But despite these rivals, Islay's star attraction just has to be the geese. You can hardly drive more than a few hundred yards along the road before you come across a flock of them, plucking at the grass with their powerful bills. A few years ago, the geese were the cause of an unholy row between conservationists and local farmers, who understandably resented the destruction of their precious crops. Thanks to a far-sighted scheme, however, farmers are now compensated for the presence of feeding geese on their land, and as a result the goose population is increasing – a welcome success story.

Among the vast flocks there were even a couple of unexpected visitors, both from North America. Somewhere in Arctic Greenland, a Canada Goose and a Snow Goose had managed to get themselves caught up with flocks of Barnacles and Whitefronts respectively, ending up on the wrong side of the Atlantic.

The Snow Goose likes the island so much it has returned to the same farm above Port Charlotte for the past four winters. It isn't too hard to see – standing out like a white flag among its dark-brown companions in the late afternoon gloom.

A wandering beauty

JULY 1997

I first heard the news one Sunday evening last month. I was enjoying a quiet drink with two birding friends, Clive and Audrey. Audrey comes from Shetland, so I mentioned that I was about to go filming there for the new series of *Birding with Bill Oddie*. Overhearing this, Clive put down his pint, and enquired: 'Do you know what's been found on Shetland today?' I did not. He leaned forward, and in a low voice simply said: 'Blue-cheeked Bee-eater'.

Only a hard-core birder can really appreciate the significance of those four little words. Of all the 550 or so species on the official 'British List', Blue-cheeked Bee-eater is just about the most exotic. With its long, slim body and iridescent green plumage, it is, quite simply, stunning. If there were a beauty contest for birds, it would walk it.

If you'd asked me what I was hoping to see in Shetland, I might have mentioned the vast breeding colonies of seabirds or Red-necked Phalarope, a rare and attractive wader. I might have added Arctic Tern or Arctic Skua, birds with appropriate names for these northerly latitudes. But never in a million years would I have thought of Blue-cheeked Bee-eater.

As its name suggests, the species lives on a diet of bees, a fairly scarce commodity in Shetland. Fortunately, this particular bird had the sense to take up residence in one of the very few wooded gardens, at Asta House near Scalloway. Reports suggested that it was coping well with the chill northerly winds, while making short work of the local bumblebees.

But how had it got there? After all, at this time of year it should have been breeding somewhere in North Africa or the Middle East. Clive summed it up perfectly, when he described bee-eaters as 'wanderers'. This bird had 'gone flyabout', heading further and further north on high pressure weather systems, before finally landing on this rugged archipelago only a few degrees south of the Arctic Circle.

I had wanted to see a Blue-cheeked Bee-eater for almost 30 years, when, as a boy, I first read Hilda Quick's account of finding 'a strange and wonderful bird' on the Isles of Scilly. Since then, only a few have been seen in Britain, and none has stayed longer than three days. I knew that I couldn't get to Shetland until Wednesday, by which time, no doubt, the bird would have flown away.

Wednesday morning arrived, and Bill Oddie and I flew to Shetland.

As we were waiting for the luggage at Sumburgh Airport, I rang Birdline to get the latest news. 'In Shetland, the Blue-cheeked Bee-eater is still at Asta House, north of Scalloway . . .' We leapt into the hire car and drove north, frantically trying to contact the camera crew, who were still filming on the island of Noss. The message got through, and we arrived at Asta just after they did. It was the usual story – the bee-eater had flown off 20 minutes before.

So we set up the camera and waited, as the clock ticked by. We knew we had to leave by 6.30, to travel to the island of Mousa to film the nightly spectacle of Storm Petrels arriving back at their nests. As six o'clock came and went, we had just about given up hope.

Then there was a movement at the top of a sycamore tree. I lifted my binoculars, and before my eyes was the most breathtakingly beautiful bird I have ever seen: a vision of rich, warm colours somehow out of place in this harsh, grey landscape. We stood and watched for 20 minutes, as it caught some of the biggest bumblebees I have ever seen. Then, as suddenly as it had arrived, it vanished.

And yes, we did get it on camera.

Down on the farm

 AUGUST 1997

Who'd go birdwatching on a farm – especially at the height of summer, traditionally one of the quietest times of the year for bird activity? Well, at the end of last month I did – and believe me, it was well worth it.

Once again, I was accompanied by a production team and film crew, shooting the new series of *Birding with Bill Oddie*. Our week in the heart of East Anglia coincided with yet another spell of warm, fine weather, with day after day of sunshine. Following the downpours earlier in the summer, this was welcomed by film crews, farmers and birds alike.

We began by visiting a derelict barn at Mannington Hall, north Norfolk, with Mike Toms from the BTO's Project Barn Owl. Wet weather is disastrous for Barn Owls, as they are unable to hunt in the rain, so their chicks starve to death. Fortunately, when Mike climbed a ladder to look into the nestbox he was able to confirm the presence of a female, brooding her new clutch of four eggs. I've never seen Bill move so fast – straight up the ladder to get his best ever views of a Barn Owl. We got some great shots, too – and only afterwards did I realise that I had not actually seen the owl myself. Still, I can always watch it on video afterwards.

Next evening we were near Norwich, looking for another kind of owl. Little Owls are, as their name suggests, tiny – barely the size of a thrush, although their staring yellow eyes make them appear far bigger. Farmer Chris Skinner had given us a useful tip: Little Owls prefer to face into the sun. Using this advice, our researcher soon located the owl, which was sitting in the branches of a gnarled old oak. Wildlife cameraman Andrew got his usual 'eyes and teeth' views, and we retired to a local hotel for a well-deserved rest.

But not for long. The sun rises early this far east, and we were soon out in the field again – literally. Chris Knights' farm at Gooderstone is one of the largest in the whole of East Anglia, with acres and acres of carrots and other root vegetables destined for a well-known high street supermarket. Fortunately, Chris has found a way of balancing the needs of an efficient business with those of the birds. As a result, his farm is packed with Grey and Red-legged Partridges, Tree Sparrows, Linnets and Whitethroats, most of which are declining elsewhere. Here, thanks to Chris's enlightened farming practices, they thrive.

But the star bird of Chris's farm is a real rarity. The Stone Curlew is the only European representative of an African family known as the 'thick-knees'. It is mainly nocturnal, with large, staring eyes, long legs and a mournful cry reminiscent of its commoner namesake. We spent a fruitless hour or two trying to approach the birds close enough to film them, and in the end had to use one of Chris's own photographic hides, which produced stunning results.

On the hottest day of the week we found ourselves in the wide open country of the south Lincolnshire fens. With such vast fields and total absence of hedgerows you might think there wouldn't be many birds to see. But first impressions can be misleading. Drainage dykes act as hedge substitutes, and a few patches of carefully planted set-aside create valuable pockets of breeding habitat.

Nick Watts' farm at Deeping St Nicholas supports thriving populations of all three farmland buntings: Corn, Reed and Yellowhammer. Their songs echo over the flat landscape: the 'jangling keys' of the Corn Bunting, the 'one-two-testing' of the Reed, and the classic sound of the Yellowhammer – usually written down as 'a-little-bit-of-bread-and-no-cheeeeeese'. True to form, Bill came up with a saucier version, the reply of a young maiden about to lose her virtue to a horny-handed son of toil: 'no-no-no-no-no-pleeeeeaaaase'.

CHAPTER 3

My local patch

1994–1997

Every birder needs a place they can call their own – somewhere they can visit on a regular basis and get to know the local birdlife. Until 1994 I lived in an area of north London where the only birds I saw were confined to the park pond; hardly inspiring even to the most dedicated urban birder. Having moved to south-west London, I cast my eye around for somewhere suitable – and when my car broke down on the way to work one day, I found it.

While waiting for the AA to arrive I took a stroll down a narrow path leading down to the Thames in Barnes. Once a year, the towpath here is thronged with rowing enthusiasts, cheering the crews of the Oxford and Cambridge Boat Race. But on this day at the end of July it was quiet and peaceful, and I discovered one of London's best-kept ornithological secrets: Lonsdale Road Reservoir.

Over the next three years or so I was a faithful visitor to what soon became 'my local patch'. In that time I recorded a grand total of 89 species: nothing out of the ordinary, but including enough 'goodies' to keep me interested. All in all, I made almost 300 visits to Lonsdale Road, which given the relative lack of unusual birds may seem a trifle excessive. So what kept me going? The best way to describe a birder's relationship with a local patch is that the more you go, the more you want to return. Somehow the very act of getting to know somewhere and its birds in minute detail reinforces the pleasure and interest you derive from each visit.

It was the break-up of my marriage, and a move elsewhere, that took me away from my patch. Of course I missed the place, and felt the odd pang of regret at the ending of my visits there. But as the final chapter of this volume shows, I did eventually find another – even better – local patch, a few miles down the road.

Looking back, it was a memorable three years: as much for the people I met as the birds I saw. As one of them told me, in a back-handed compliment: 'I enjoy your articles; but remember, it's not just *your* patch, it's *our* patch too!'

First visit

 AUGUST 1994

A local patch can be anywhere. The top of a mountain, a coastal marsh, a city park – all have their own unique and fascinating birdlife. Of course, some patches are more productive than others, but wherever you choose, there's always something interesting going on. And as the birds come and go, from day to day and from season to season, you are on hand to witness the changes.

A recent move across London means that I have a new local patch. Lonsdale Road Reservoir lies alongside the southern bank of the River

Thames, to the west of Hammersmith Bridge in south-west London. Built by the Victorians, it has long fallen into disuse as a working reservoir and is now a local nature reserve.

It may not rival more glamorous sites, but it still has a lot going for it. It is small – about half-a-mile long and a hundred yards wide – and self-contained. The lake itself is ringed by a footpath giving good views of the water, so you can cover the area thoroughly with just a pair of binoculars, instead of the vast array of optical equipment carried by some of today's birdwatchers.

Much favoured by dog-walkers, duck-feeders and courting couples, Lonsdale Road has another advantage: the birds are used to people, so are quite happy to sit still and be counted. This means that comparisons can be made and changes documented, providing a small but useful set of statistics in the battle for bird conservation.

So what birds are found here? Well, as you might expect from a former reservoir, waterfowl predominate. On my first visit at the end of July, Mallards, Tufted Ducks, Coots and Moorhens were all present with young. I also saw Great Crested and Little Grebes, along with a few Cormorants, drying their wings after fishing in the nearby river.

My first surprise was a family party of the notorious Ruddy Duck, including three males, sporting their russet plumage and bright blue bills. A few days later I discovered a female with no fewer than seven tiny chicks, obviously hatched only a day or two earlier. Whichever side of the Ruddy Duck debate you favour (and I am, I must confess, a defender of this alien upstart), it is hard not to enjoy such a sight.

At this time of year, of course, the place is full of young birds – from the Reed Warblers at the northern end of the lake, to the Song Thrushes and Blackbirds in the brambles along the footpath. However, after their young have fledged most birds stop singing, so the patch can appear rather lacking in birdlife, especially during the middle of the day.

But if I'm lucky, an early-morning visit may still be brightened up by the blue-and-orange flash of a Kingfisher, as it flicks from branch to branch along the water's edge. And the evening sees flocks of House Martins and a few Swifts hawking for flies, with the occasional Common Tern passing through.

Despite the current heatwave, it won't be long before these birds travel south to spend the winter in Africa. As they depart, and the lush summer vegetation begins to thin out, the ducks will emerge from their dull 'eclipse plumage' into their full finery, in preparation for the autumn and winter.

Over the coming year, in this monthly column, I shall be following the fortunes of this little patch of riverside suburbia. I aim to document the changes, the arrivals and departures, and with luck, perhaps tell you about a few surprises. In the meantime, I'd better wander over for my daily visit. I wonder what will turn up this morning?

Arrivals and departures

SEPTEMBER 1994

It's been just over a month now since I began to visit my new local patch. Yet already I am beginning to understand the rhythms and patterns of its birdlife. Take the locals. On regular visits, you don't just get to know familiar species, but the individuals themselves. Ever-present birds include a family party of eight Mute Swans, which have a nasty habit of harassing passers-by for food. Other regulars include a single Grey Heron, usually standing on one of the small artificial islands in the centre of the lake.

Then there are the Ruddy Duck chicks, the fourth brood here this year. These hatched around mid-August, and a couple of weeks later had dwindled in number from seven to just four. The unfortunate trio could perhaps have been taken by pike, but a more exotic culprit may have been responsible.

One sunny day last month, I glanced down at the sun-bleached branches of a fallen tree, poking out of the algae-covered water. There, sunning themselves like a platoon of beached submarines, were three Red-eared Terrapins. A passing jogger told me that they arrived here at the height of the Ninja Turtle craze of a few years ago. Presumably the owners, terrified by the terrapins' ability to eat almost anything within range of their powerful jaws, liberated them into this quiet backwater.

Whether or not Ruddy Duck chicks are on the menu, the terrapins appear to be holding their own. Some have grown to the size of dinner-plates, and with their chrome-yellow, green and black coloration, set off by the tiny red spot behind each ear, they make an interesting addition to the capital's fauna.

In the meantime, the local birdlife has undergone some changes, as summer passes inexorably into autumn. Duck numbers began to build up through August, with up to 40 Pochard joining the usual Tufted Ducks. Parties of Shovelers, their massive bill sifting the water surface for tiny morsels of food, have already come and gone, with the bulk passing through in the last fortnight of August. Three tiny Teal also frequented the shallows at the southern end for a day or two at that time.

Casual visitors are few and far between on the patch, perhaps because its enclosure by trees prevents migrants and other passers-by from dropping in. Nevertheless, a visiting Sparrowhawk was mobbed by a local crow, while one evening a Common Sandpiper fed along the exposed bank.

In the bird calendar, autumn is already well under way, and I don't expect to see the local Reed Warblers again until next spring. My last sighting was on the final day of August, and these tiny skulkers are now on their way to their wintering grounds south of the Sahara. Meanwhile, there are the first signs of the season to come. Tit flocks are beginning to build up, with the occasional Long-tailed Tit joining the more familiar species as they pass through the foliage, chattering and scolding as they go.

Yet even by mid-September, summer isn't quite over. As the chill winds of autumn gather strength, a pair of Great Crested Grebes has chosen to raise a final brood of chicks. The adults are currently sitting on a nest built on the edge of a reedbed. But will they win their race against time and raise their young, before winter takes its grip on the patch?

Starting them young

OCTOBER 1994

I recently took an early-morning stroll around my local patch. It was a cool, cloudy day, with a fresh north-easterly wind – not the ideal conditions for raising young birds. Yet despite the autumnal weather and the late date, the resident pair of Great Crested Grebes had just managed to hatch three chicks.

With their striped plumage and ungainly shape, grebe chicks are in sharp contrast to their elegant parents. They spend a lot of time out of the water – not along the banks of the reservoir, but on their parents' backs. The adult bird glides along the surface of the water like a square-rigger in full sail, accompanied by three tiny heads poking out from its ruffled plumage. Meanwhile, its partner dives constantly for the tiny silver-coloured fish which appear to be the chicks' staple diet.

During the course of the month, the grebe chicks have grown rapidly, more than doubling in size and weight. After a fortnight or so I was surprised to notice a fourth, slightly smaller chick. I can only presume that this bird must have been hidden among its parents' feathers all along. The good news is that despite the very late date, all four chicks have so far survived both the colder weather and the danger from predators.

I have a soft spot for Great Crested Grebes, as I used to watch them when I was a child, on the disused gravel-pits along the River Thames at Shepperton. I can still remember the excitement of climbing along a branch over the water with my friend Ian Hyde, to find my first grebe's nest. It contained three elongated, pale eggs, stained olive-green by the waterweed used to cover them by the parent birds. Despite a youthful desire to collect anything and everything, I'm pleased to report that we left the eggs untouched.

A quarter of a century later, I can now watch nesting Great Crested Grebes with my two young sons, David and James. The patch is an ideal place to do this, being a kind of natural adventure playground, complete with trees for climbing, stones for throwing, and sticks to beat down stinging nettles. Of course, I have to contend with the problems faced by every modern parent: the children's inability to walk more than 200 yards without complaining; their tendency to fall off trees; and their constant need to express excitement at full volume. Nevertheless, on an hour's walk last Sunday, we did manage to see 30 different species of bird. We were helped by the calm, sunny weather, which brought back memories of the long-departed summer and encouraged constant activity among the birds.

The summer visitors are long gone now, of course, but their place has been taken by a gradual inflow of birds planning to spend the winter in the area. A small flock of gulls, mostly Black-headed but with the odd Common and Lesser Black-backed, has joined the ducks at feeding-time. Meanwhile, Wrens, Robins and Blue Tits hunt for insects along the lakeside bushes and trees.

The highlight of our walk was a close-up view of a female Sparrowhawk, which flew low over our heads and off towards nearby gardens, in search of birdtables attracting its songbird prey. David and James were more interested in the possibility of paddling at the water's edge, and that's perhaps how it should be.

After all, enthusiasm for the natural world can only develop through experience, gained first hand somewhere like this. Our little patch of wilderness in the midst of suburbia is just one of thousands of places in Britain where children and adults can enjoy the sights and sounds of wild nature. Long may it remain.

A wise old owl

 DECEMBER 1994

My fears back in September for the newly hatched grebe chicks were unfounded: at least three have survived, and are now moulting out of their candy-striped juvenile costume and into the brown-and-white feathers of their first-winter. Meanwhile, the adults are stubbornly refusing to begin to moult out of breeding plumage, and are indulging in behaviour more typical of early spring than late autumn. One morning I caught a glimpse of the adult grebes 'standing up' in the water, face to face, doing their famous 'penguin dance' courtship display. If the weather holds out, who knows, we may even see them attempt to raise another brood over Christmas.

Apart from the grebes' unseasonable behaviour, it's been a fairly quiet month on the patch. Even so, numbers of winter visitors, such as the Cormorant flock, are building up. When I was growing up in the 1960s, Cormorants were just beginning to change their status from mainly coastal birds to ones that winter in good numbers inland. Helped by the proliferation of gravel-pits and reservoirs, they soon became a familiar sight around the London suburbs.

Even so, one day last month I was surprised to count 49 Cormorants resting on the artificial rafts provided for nesting ducks. More than two thirds were in the oily, greenish-black adult plumage; the rest a mixture of dirty cream and brown, indicating their juvenile status. At low tide on the nearby river, they hop over here to the reservoir, where they perch with open wings, hanging them out to dry like a gaggle of washerwomen.

I'm able to see them more easily now that the leaves have finally fallen from the dense thicket of trees and shrubs which encircles the reservoir. The coming of winter also makes it much easier to see the smaller wintering species, such as Long-tailed Tits, Chiffchaffs and Goldcrests. Even so, I usually hear these birds before I see them, as they call incessantly in order to communicate with the rest of their flock.

The lack of foliage also helped me to find a new bird for the patch this month. One of the tall trees alongside the River Thames has a hole in its trunk. Blocking the hole was what at first sight looked like a pile of brown, autumn leaves, but on closer inspection revealed itself to be more animate – though only slightly. It was a Tawny Owl, roosting during the daylight hours in its south-facing niche, which on fine days enables it to bask in the warmth of the winter sun.

Unlike most other species of birds, which flee the worst of harsh winter weather, the owl prefers to adopt a wait-and-see strategy. Instead of moving on at the first sight of ice and snow, it stays put on its familiar breeding territory, adapting its diet to more catholic fare, even including earthworms. In doing so, it takes advantage of local knowledge and expends less energy, often enabling Tawny Owls to survive cold spells better than their wandering relatives.

Perhaps birdwatchers could learn a lesson from the Tawny Owl. Spending the winter covering one small area thoroughly is likely to be more rewarding than chasing up and down the country after rare visitors, and it's a lot less hassle.

New Year freeze

 JANUARY 1995

The nice thing about my local patch is that it provides an oasis of peace and quiet in the midst of city life. Apart from the distant hum of traffic, and the occasional whiff of hops from the nearby Mortlake brewery, it's hard to believe that you're just a few miles from London's West End.

Bordered by housing estates on one side and the River Thames on the other, the patch also provides a welcome haven for birds, where they can feed, rest and spend the winter months in comfort. Until, that is, the weather intervenes. The cold snap around the New Year brought some noticeable changes to the birdlife here. As the water began to freeze for the first time since I began my visits, I awaited the outcome with keen interest. I certainly wasn't disappointed.

The most conspicuous new arrivals are the ducks. One early morning, at the height of the freeze-up, I counted 130 Tufted Ducks and more than 180 Shovelers, huddled together on the narrow strip of ice-free water in the centre of the lake. Shovelers are a regular autumn and winter sight here, living up to their name by ploughing their massive bills through the surface of the water to find their tiny invertebrate prey. As the waters froze, concentrating so many birds in such a small area, they looked almost like a single organism, moving in unison across the water in search of food.

The hard weather brought some unexpected new arrivals. Small flocks of Reed Buntings now haunt the patches of reeds around the lake, and a Grey Wagtail spends the early mornings searching for insect food along the concrete banks. Few birds are so badly named as this species, one of the most beautiful of all British birds. More slender and graceful than the commoner Pied Wagtail, the Grey Wagtail's slate-grey and yellow plumage and high-pitched call are guaranteed to draw attention – and not just from birdwatchers. This particular bird's arrival has given rise to territorial jealousy, with the resident Pied Wagtail chasing it away as soon as it dares to alight.

The cold weather has made the wintering flocks of Great, Blue and Long-tailed Tits even more confiding, and they can often be watched without binoculars as they feed just a couple of feet in front of my eyes. With them one day was a male Blackcap, a robust, greyish-brown warbler. Until recently the Blackcap was almost unknown in winter in the British Isles. In the last few years, however, birds from central Europe have begun to change their migratory habits. Like their close relative, the Chiffchaff, some Blackcaps have discovered that it pays to forgo the long and dangerous migratory journey south in favour of a shorter movement westwards, to the relatively mild winter climate of the British Isles.

So instead of heading south-west towards Spain or North Africa, each autumn they hop across the Channel to spend the winter closer to home. Blackcaps are now regular visitors to birdtables, and a female bird (with a brown, rather than black, cap) spent Christmas in and around my own garden. If the present run of mild winters continues, especially in south-east England, we may even begin to see other summer visitors staying on here. Even that familiar proverb, 'one swallow doesn't make a summer', may eventually become redundant.

In the meantime, as the cold snap recedes, life on the patch is getting back to normal. Soon the courtship rituals which mark the beginning of the breeding season will begin. In the middle of winter it's a cheering thought to consider another familiar proverb: 'If winter comes, can spring be far behind?'

The aliens are here

 MARCH 1995

The aliens are here. No, not little green men, but big, green parakeets. Originally imported as cagebirds, then released back in the 1960s and 1970s, flocks of this Indian invader are now a regular sight around the south-west London suburbs. There, they find rich pickings among the ornamental parks and gardens.

So I wasn't surprised on a sunny morning last month when I heard a foreign but familiar screeching in the trees above my head. Looking up, I saw a lone Ring-necked Parakeet, an elegant, lime-green bird with a ludicrously long tail. This first bird was obviously on a recce: taking a look around my local patch to see if there were any holes suitable for nesting. Despite attracting the hostility of a Magpie, he soon found one – then with a series of high-pitched calls, flew off across the River Thames.

A week or so later he was back with his mates – flying around their new territory like the birding equivalent of lager louts. Now up to five parakeets have taken up residence – much to the astonishment of the local crows, who frequently mob these unwelcome upstarts as they pass overhead.

Introduced species such as the Ring-necked Parakeet are often highly successful, mainly because they have several advantages over natives. First, they can exploit a vacant ecological niche, thus avoiding competition with other species. Second, they don't have any natural predators, so their populations often increase geometrically. Recently almost 700 parakeets were counted as they went to roost at a site by the River Thames at Walton.

In fact, alien species make up a substantial proportion of the birds seen at the patch. Of the sixty or so species I've recorded so far, no fewer than six are aliens – a ratio of one in ten. This is perhaps because introduced species tend to thrive in man-made habitats, and close to large areas of population, where food is more easily obtainable. This is certainly true of the most populous species: the Canada Goose, and also appears to hold for two more recent invaders, the parakeet and the Ruddy Duck.

Of course, most birds on the patch are still pukka, native British species. These include two welcome returners, a regular pair of Kestrels. They have taken to sitting on a branch just above the footpath, giving tremendous views, and neatly illustrating their difference in size – the female being appreciably bulkier than her mate. Together with a more elusive pair of Sparrowhawks, they seem likely to settle down to breed at Lonsdale Road.

And they're not the only ones. Mild, spring weather has encouraged all the local birds to start forming pairs and defending territories for the breeding season to come. March gives the resident species a chance to get a head start on their migrant counterparts, and by the end of the month the first chicks should have begun to fledge. Early spring is a great time to practise your skills at identifying birdsong, especially while the foliage isn't yet fully grown, so you can still see the singing birds. If you're really keen, then you can get hold of tapes or CDs to help you practise.

But if you want to learn the call of the Ring-necked Parakeet, you won't find it on any of the usual recordings. Fortunately, that's not really a problem – like everything else about this new arrival, its high-pitched screeching is, quite simply, unforgettable.

A bird's-eye view

 JUNE 1995

Last month, after ten days birdwatching in Hungary, I passed over south-west London on the approach to Heathrow. Looking down, I caught sight of my local patch, hugging the bank of the River Thames alongside the Boat Race course between Hammersmith and Chiswick. For a moment I had, quite literally, a bird's-eye view of the place. A little strip of fresh water, surrounded by the lush greenery of spring. If I'd been a passing bird, instead of an airline passenger, I think I would have been tempted to drop in and see what was on offer.

But if it hadn't been for a small group of dedicated people and a far-sighted local council, all I would have seen would have been a housing estate or playing fields. A few years ago this disused reservoir was derelict, vandalised and under threat from development. Fortunately the local people got together with Richmond Council and created a nature reserve, preserving the site for newcomers like me to enjoy.

On most visits, I come across one of the people who campaigned for the reserve. For almost 30 years, Violet Hoare has taken a daily walk around the banks of Lonsdale Road Reservoir. She feeds the ducks, picks up litter and, despite failing eyesight, still manages to see most of the local birdlife. Violet regards the birds as 'hers' and protects them with a fierce determination.

Fortunately for Violet and the rest of the regular visitors, it's been a good breeding season. Despite the usual disturbance from the kids who use the place as an adventure playground, a pair of Mute Swans has once again managed to raise young – five well-grown cygnets. Two Common Terns have returned from Africa, and with luck will breed on one of the artificial islands in the middle of the lake. Meanwhile Coots, Moorhens and Mallards are producing chicks like they're going out of fashion.

Britain is full of wonderful places like this: surrounded by suburban sprawl or what passes for 'countryside' in these days of intensive agriculture. Sadly, many of them are now under threat of development. Not far away in south London, the former sewage farm at Beddington faces destruction, because of Thames Water's plans to turn it into a waste landfill site.

It's not only the human residents who are concerned about this. For years Beddington has been a welcome haven for migrating and wintering birds, especially waders, ducks and the declining Tree Sparrow. Even as you read this, localised breeding species such as Yellow Wagtail and Lapwing are raising their young there.

Of course in a decade or two, when the site is full of rubbish and has been landscaped, there will still be birds at Beddington. But they'll be those species that thrive in the company of humans, such as gulls and crows. The variety of species, which is what makes Beddington so special, will have gone, never to return. Another local patch will have been lost forever.

A more sympathetic development is going on elsewhere in the capital, at Barn Elms Reservoirs, near Hammersmith. There, on the site of four disused reservoirs, the Wildfowl and Wetlands Trust is creating its first urban wildlife centre. By the turn of the new century west London will hopefully have a site to rival anywhere in southern England, with purpose-built wetland habitats to attract a variety of breeding, migrating and wintering birds. It doesn't take much to see the educational possibilities of somewhere like that in the very heart of the city – a place for birds and people alike.

Fortunately, Beddington was saved from the developers and remains one of the foremost birding sites in London.

One year on

 JULY 1995

It's almost a year since I first went to Lonsdale Road Reservoir and began writing about its birds. I can still remember the excitement of that very first visit – when I turned off a busy road to discover a little patch of green in the heart of the London suburbs. Since then I've made almost a hundred visits: at different times of the day, during different seasons, and in all kinds of weather. I've recorded 66 species of birds, a modest total compared with more extensive or better-placed sites, but still impressive for a limited habitat on the edge of London.

Of these 66 species, more than 35 have bred – underlining the importance of sites like this for conservation. A further dozen or so species are predominately winter visitors, including good numbers of duck, and a large flock of roosting Cormorants. Some are summer migrants, like the Swifts and House Martins which nest nearby. The rest are casual visitors, either dropping in to feed for a few hours or passing overhead.

The best season to visit Lonsdale Road is undoubtedly late winter or early spring – not least because with the leaves off the trees, you can get a good view of the water. On a typical early morning visit, before the birds have been disturbed too much, you should see a good variety of species.

As you'd expect, the bias is heavily in favour of waterbirds, with two species of grebe and several species of duck, as well as the ever-present Mute Swans, Moorhens and Coots. There is also a good selection of songbirds in the trees and bushes around the lake. Wintering Chiffchaffs, Blackcaps, Goldcrests and Long-tailed Tits are all regular, and often amazingly tame. And there's always a chance of seeing some of the more interesting residents, including Kestrels and Sparrowhawks, Great Spotted Woodpeckers, and a recent arrival – the Ring-necked Parakeet.

For most birdwatchers who visit the patch, the year's highlight was the roosting Tawny Owl, discovered in November, and more or less constantly present until the end of March. Other unusual visitors included a Common Sandpiper in August, a party of Pintails in January, and the occasional Kingfisher – a welcome sight on several autumn mornings.

From a mammal-lover's point of view, the patch is less rewarding: Grey Squirrels and Brown Rats being the two most prominent residents. However, the colony of Red-eared Terrapins, basking on the branches of a fallen tree trunk, is a sight worth seeing.

In the past year, I've met all sorts of people during my visits: bird-watchers, dog-walkers, joggers, courting couples – and just curious passers-by. Some visit every single day, others call in just once in a while. But for all of them, this little place is somewhere special.

Environmentalists are always banging on about the need to conserve places like this for future generations to enjoy. Well, they happen to be right. Knowing that there is somewhere I can escape for an hour or so before work or at the weekend is really important to me. And I'm sure I'm not alone.

Violet

 NOVEMBER 1995

It's finally happened. The leaves have turned golden-brown, the temperature has dropped and, at last, autumn has arrived. And with the change in the season, the birds make changes, too. Tiny Goldcrests come together in flocks to feed, their peeping call barely audible to the human ear; wintering gulls noisily scavenge for food; and, as their young reach full size, the resident Great Crested Grebes begin to lose their breeding finery and take on a more muted plumage in preparation for the coming winter.

But as I take my journey around the footpath that encircles the patch, there is something missing. The birds know it, especially the ducks, which are no longer fed each morning. The people – at least those like me who are regular visitors – know it, too. The redoubtable Miss Violet Hoare, the woman who more than any other saved Lonsdale Road Reservoir from development, will no longer take her daily pilgrimage around its banks.

I heard the news back in late September. Violet had died peacefully in her sleep, having never missed a day's visit to the place that became her second home. Every morning for almost 30 years, she took her walk and greeted familiar faces and strangers alike with the same cheery smile.

Violet knew the patch long before it gained official status as a local nature reserve. She knew its comings and goings – the regular seasonal changes of personnel as birds departed south or arrived from the north. In her later years she became deaf, and felt keenly her inability to hear birdsong, though perhaps she didn't miss the accompanying sounds from jumbo jets passing overhead on their way to land at Heathrow.

We would meet at the little bay along the eastern bank, where the ducks, geese, coots and swans competed for Violet's attention as she distributed the day's food. She was always keen to know of any unusual sightings, and often pointed out particular birds to me, such as the three Pintails that dropped in during a cold spell last winter.

At her funeral service, held on a bright, warm day at the end of September, we learnt that Violet had, like many people, a past life that few of us knew about. She had been a senior manager for a French firm in London, and for her services to the Free French during the war had been awarded a medal of honour. No doubt the ducks, swans and others that she kept fed and safe would award her a medal, too, if they could. After the service I wandered across the road to the patch and sat quietly for a few minutes. Everything was as it should be: the grebes fed their ever-hungry young, Robins and Wrens sang in the undergrowth, and a more recent arrival, a Ring-necked Parakeet, screeched in the branches overhead.

I reflected that without Violet, and the other dedicated people who worked so hard to save the reservoir, this place would probably now be under tons of concrete. It seems a fitting memorial to an extraordinary woman.

Two years on

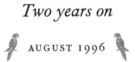

AUGUST 1996

Can it really be only two years since I first visited my local patch? Some mornings, as I walk or cycle along the narrow path around the reservoir and watch the bird activity, it seems as if I've been coming here forever. This is partly down to the comforting familiarity of everyday landmarks. There's the little reedbed at the north end, summer home for a couple of pairs of Reed Warblers. The patch of sallows at the southern end, where I always hope to come across some scarce migrant, but never do. And the row of old Black Poplar trees, so late to come into leaf this spring.

Every birdwatcher enjoys coming across the unexpected. But one of the best things about making regular visits to your local patch is the usual birds: the resident pair of Mute Swans, the arrival of the first Swifts in spring or the flocks of wintering Shovelers in autumn. Even the customary flock of Carrion Crows, squabbling noisily in the trees by the gate, are a welcome sight.

I suppose it's not really surprising that I find the sights and sounds of this place familiar. I have, after all, made almost 200 visits there since July 1994. Why? What's the point in going to one place so many times, especially when it is just one of thousands of ordinary sites up and down the country? Well, apart from the fact I enjoy being out in the fresh air (always the standard birder's excuse), it's because even a small, land-locked location like this can turn up a surprising number of different kinds of birds.

So far, I've recorded 80 species at Lonsdale Road – either resting on the water, feeding in the surrounding bushes and trees or simply flying overhead. In the past year, I've added just over a baker's dozen to my list – 14 species I didn't see during my first year on the patch.

Some of these are commonplace birds elsewhere – but locally rare in this particular part of the London suburbs. They include sightings of Jackdaws and Wigeon – hardly likely to cause a mass twitch. Nevertheless, to me they were as exciting as any storm-driven rarity. For these were my birds.

There were also a few more memorable sightings, such as the female Wheatear I almost ran over on the road outside, one sunny April morning. The Water Rail I saw on Boxing Day, which scuttled into the reeds when it caught sight of me, never to be seen again. And no fewer than three species of woodpecker – the entire British contingent – all of which attempted to breed in the poplar trees alongside the River Thames.

The year's 'purple patch' came in late April and early May, when despite the chilly weather I added no fewer than ten species to my Lonsdale Road list, including an acrobatic Hobby. During the course of the spring I also recorded seven different species of warbler, each filling the morning air with song, as if to celebrate a safe return from their African winter-quarters.

In the end, the real joy in patch-watching is the knowledge that I am helping to create a permanent record of the birdlife of one tiny corner of the British Isles. It may not be a famous place for birds, like Minsmere or Cley, nor a remote or majestic one, like Fair Isle or the Cairngorms. But it is still a place where birds come and go, act out the dramas of their daily lives, and continually enthral at least one person passionate about birdwatching.

New Year again

 JANUARY 1997

The other day, as I was cycling along the riverfront at Barnes, I caught sight of a blue plaque on the front of a terraced house – 'Gustav Holst, Composer, lived here: 1908-1913'. I have no idea how many birds Holst would have seen from his front window, during a quick break from composing. Nowadays there are usually a few gulls, a Mallard or two and perhaps a Cormorant drying its wings at the water's edge.

But this winter has been different. As ponds, lakes and reservoirs froze right across the south-east, the tidal Thames has been a welcome refuge for hungry birds. Although harsh winter weather is usually bad news for birds, it's often good news for birdwatchers, and the recent cold spell was no exception.

My car broke down on Christmas Eve, and for the whole of the holiday period I was reliant on bus and bicycle, and confined to local birding. So I took advantage of both to visit the riverfront regularly.

One bright, cold day, on a visit with six-year-old James and his classmate Sam, we counted a thousand gulls feeding on the exposed mud at low tide. Most were winter-plumage Black-headed, sporting a small black dot behind the eye instead of the dark hood of their breeding dress. There were also good numbers of plump Common Gulls (once described to me as 'looking like they'd be better to eat than the Black-headed') and a handful of predatory Lesser Black-backed and Herring Gulls. The other contender for most numerous bird was the ubiquitous Canada Goose. As a flock of several hundred flew honking over my head at dusk one evening, I could almost imagine myself on a windswept, lonely estuary. Well, almost.

Among the usual flock of Mallards were a score of Teal: Britain's smallest duck, and with its rich chestnut and green head markings, one of our most attractive. Along the riverbank itself there were some unexpected visitors: a splendid male Goosander, and a small flock of Redshank and Dunlin, refugees from the coast.

On New Year's Day, Neil McKillop and I continued our long tradition of rising before dawn to race round the London suburbs – in search of birds, of course. We didn't quite break our all-time record of 71 species, but still managed a very respectable 69, including Smew, Black-necked Grebe, and two introduced aliens, Mandarin Duck and Ring-necked Parakeet.

The best bird of the day came at an unlikely spot: the railway station at Wraysbury. We'd just got back to the car and were enjoying a warming drink, when I noticed a fellow birder watching intently from a tiny bridge over the frozen stream. I wandered over, and he pointed just below the bridge. About ten yards away, a Bittern stood motionless, with its bill pointing in the air. This was probably a bird from the Continent, forced to flee westwards in search of milder weather. Sadly for the Bittern, it had so far failed in its quest.

We watched for a minute or two, when suddenly the bird took a couple of steps forward and disappeared swiftly into a tiny clump of reeds. At that moment, another birder appeared, and we had the unpleasant duty of breaking the news of what he'd just missed.

You always feel better after seeing a bird like a Bittern, and for the rest of the day we walked around like the Ready Brek kids, cocooned in an aura of warmth and well-being.

The wonder of gulls

 OCTOBER 1997

Almost five years ago, I wrote my very first 'Birdwatch' column on the subject of gulls. Not, perhaps, the most glamorous or exciting group of birds – until, that is, you take a closer look. In fact, gulls are among the most fascinating, intelligent and adaptable of all wild birds.

They are often labelled with the convenient but inaccurate term, 'seagulls'. A century or so ago, when gulls were mainly marine birds, that would have been perfectly acceptable. But since then, things have changed dramatically. Nowadays gulls spend much of their lives inland, finding rich pickings among the discarded refuse from our own wasteful lifestyles. During the spring and summer most head north to their breeding colonies. But by early autumn, they begin to return and are a familiar sight in most towns and cities throughout the winter months.

One Sunday morning last month I took my son James and his friend Sam to have a look at the gulls on my local patch. I was showing them how to tell a Black-headed apart from a Common Gull, when another bird flew down to land on the mud. Even at a glance, something wasn't quite right – it was noticeably darker than either of the other two species and had a black mask and a heavy, drooping black bill. I raised my binoculars and to my surprise realised it was a first-winter plumage Mediterranean Gull.

South-west London is a long way from the delights of the Med – so what was this bird doing here? In fact, despite its name, the Mediterranean Gull breeds in scattered locations throughout Europe – including France, Belgium and the Netherlands. In the last 20 years it has even managed to establish a small breeding population here in Britain, mainly among colonies of Black-headed Gulls.

So this bird could, I suppose, have come from almost any direction – north, west, east or south! If I could have got close enough to read the small metal ring around its left leg I might have discovered a clue to its origins. Unfortunately, I didn't have my telescope with me, and when I came back later the bird had disappeared. With luck, however, it will return. Gulls are creatures of habit, and at this time of year they gather together in flocks, usually in the area where they plan to spend the rest of the winter.

By Christmas there could be as many as a thousand gulls down on the riverfront, but at the moment, there are only a hundred or so. Yet the day I found the Mediterranean Gull there were no fewer than seven different species to be seen. The vast majority were Black-headed, along with a few Common and Lesser Black-backed. But as I walked along the towpath towards Hammersmith Bridge, I noticed a couple of Herring Gulls, and an adult Great Black-backed – a massive, marine gull fairly scarce this far inland.

There were also two birds which until recently might have gone unnoticed. These were Yellow-legged Gulls: distinguished from the superficially similar Herring Gull by their smaller size, darker grey back and wings, and bright yellow legs. Despite their obvious differences, until recently the Yellow-legged Gull was considered to be merely a race of the Herring Gull. Today, however, most birders consider the Yellow-legged to be a separate species.

Like the Mediterranean Gull, it also breeds south of here, on the Atlantic coast of France, and disperses widely after nesting. In recent years it has become an increasingly regular autumn and winter visitor to southern England – and earlier this year I even saw a pair breeding at a secret site on the south coast. So over the next few months I shall keep a close eye on the gulls along the riverfront. Who knows, something even rarer might turn up.

CHAPTER 4

Birding Britain

1998–2005

B y the late 1990s I had come through my mid-life crisis, and it was time to do some serious birding again. I'd also met (and in 2001 married) Suzanne, who came on a 'Spring Birding' course I was leading for the Field Studies Council. The cryptic reference at the end of the first piece in this chapter was her first appearance in a 'Birdwatch' column. Many of the accounts that follow reflect the new way in which I had begun to look at birds, with the aid of her fresh imagination, insight and enthusiasm.

Other things changed during this period, too. The annual British Birdwatching Fair became an ever more important event in our lives: a time of recreation and renewal, at which a global community of people come together for a three-day celebration of our shared passion for birds. A truly remarkable event: if you haven't ever been, then make sure you do!

As well as recreational birding, I continued to travel around Britain while making programmes with Bill Oddie: at first for three series of *Birding*; then three more of *Bill Oddie Goes Wild*; and finally for *How to Watch Wildlife* and *Springwatch*. Making television programmes about birds isn't always as exciting as it sounds: you spend more time with the camera crew than you do with the wildlife, and there's an awful lot of what a colleague of mine calls 'endless, pointless, hanging around for something to happen – God knows what!'

Nevertheless, during this period, I did manage to visit some of the very best of British wildlife sites: from Speyside to Shetland and Devon to Minsmere. I even managed a trip to the most remote – and surely the most incredible – place in Britain: the fabled islands of St Kilda. Thanks to the decision to broaden our approach to include other wildlife, I also began to take notice of other wild creatures: notably dragonflies and butterflies. Now I know what it's like to be a beginner again!

Away from it all

 JULY 1998

> Few people in this overcrowded country have not some favourite heath or common or moor to which they retire when they need solitude, or unpolluted fresh air, the glimpse of wild life, or the sound of water falling over stones.

These words, by the English landscape expert W.G. Hoskins, are as true today as when he wrote them more than a generation ago. Hoskins understood that human beings will always need special places where they are able to contemplate the natural world.

One Sunday afternoon in June, I suddenly felt the need to escape from my busy urban surroundings and to get a dose of solitude, wildlife and unpolluted fresh air. So I got into the car and headed down the A3: through the suburban blight of Tolworth, past the horrors of the M25 and into deepest Surrey.

Despite being so close to London, Surrey is still quite rural, and you can usually get away from the madding crowd. Unfortunately, on this sunny summer's evening, the madding crowd had brought their dogs, children and loud voices to the car park at Thursley Common. Fortunately, people who come in cars don't usually go very far, and I only had to walk through the wood and out onto the open common to be alone.

Well, almost alone. Thursley isn't always the easiest place to see birds, but in late June it is at its peak. Skylarks sang high in the sky above – do they ever stop for a rest? A Meadow Pipit launched into the air and parachuted down to Earth, singing as it fell. And a family of Stonechats clicked and whistled from the tops of the gorse bushes.

Thursley has its special birds, too, if you know where to look. I headed along the boardwalk, taking care not to step off into the boggy surroundings. Suddenly there was a sound of terrified quacking, and a dark object shot overhead. The noise came from a panicking pair of Mallards, and the dark shape was a pursuing Hobby.

Hobbies are far too small to catch a Mallard – but they can still give them a nasty scare. The slender, swift-like falcon whipped across the common, then rose high in the sky, where it attracted the attentions of a passing crow. The two birds made a few casual jabs at one another, before the Hobby disappeared as quickly as it had come.

Further on, a little copse of pine trees echoed to the sound of birds. Chaffinches sang, doing their usual impression of a fast bowler running up to deliver. Coal Tits and Goldcrests seeped their high-pitched calls, and in the distance, a Green Woodpecker lolloped off, laughing as it went.

By now it was almost seven o'clock, and the sun was low in the sky, bathing the gorse and heather in a golden light. I had one final quest: to see the elusive Dartford Warbler. Then I heard a short, unassuming song, like someone scratching the strings of an out-of-tune cello. I raised my binoculars just in time to see a tiny, burgundy-coloured bird dive into the foliage.

The song began again, and then stopped. The bird leapt out of the bush and bounded across to another, where for just a few seconds, it sat in full view. Unmistakably a Dartford Warbler, once one of Britain's rarest breeding birds, but thanks to the recent run of mild winters, now quite common in its specialised heathland habitat. This cheeky little bird, with its dark magenta plumage and cocked tail, is always a treat to see.

It was time to go. For one brief moment I had shared the life of a bird. In some strange, indefinable way, I had also shared the experience with every other birdwatcher that has ever seen a Dartford Warbler. And with one other special person, whose being there made the evening one I shall never forget.

The Birdfair

 AUGUST 1998

For many birdwatchers, including myself, the coming weekend sees the highlight of the birding year: the British Birdwatching Fair at Rutland Water. For three days, thousands of birdwatchers from all over Britain will converge on this tiny county in the heart of England. They'll be joined by visitors from as far apart as Israel and Costa Rica, Uganda and Trinidad & Tobago, united by one simple thing: their shared love of birds and birdwatching.

So what will they find there? Well, there are huge marquees with stalls selling everything from binoculars to exotic foreign holidays; lectures and quizzes; artists and photographers; and all sorts of local and national conservation groups. And when you've had enough, there's even a beer tent!

In the unlikely event of becoming bored, you can always go off and watch the birds. For the Birdfair, as it is usually known, doesn't take place in some vast, cavernous hall by a motorway junction, but on a really excellent bird reserve. By late August the autumn migration is well under way, and the place will be packed with birds: ducks and geese, grebes and Cormorants, and the tamest Tree Sparrows I've ever seen. At this time of year, almost anything can turn up: perhaps even an Osprey stopping off on its long journey south from Scotland to Africa.

The Birdfair has become so much a part of today's birding scene that it seems to have been going for ever. Yet the whole thing began only a decade ago, when two local conservationists, Tim Appleton and Martin Davies, came up with a bright idea. It started small, but just kept on growing, and this year marks the tenth annual fair.

Their second bright idea was to donate the profits from the Birdfair to conservation projects around the world. Over the years, more than £300,000 has been raised for projects in places like Poland, Spain, Morocco and Ecuador. This year's fair supports a project with a difference: the BirdLife International Threatened Birds Programme, which aims to create survival action plans for the world's 1111 endangered bird species, as well as raising awareness of the plight of the 10 per cent of the world's birds currently threatened with extinction.

But although it's a good thing that the Birdfair supports such worthwhile causes, that's not what makes it such fun. For me, the most important element of all is the human one. When I went to my first Birdfair, back in 1992, I only knew a handful of people there. In those days, birdwatchers tended to keep themselves to themselves, and there were few opportunities to socialise and get to know each other.

To a large extent, the Birdfair has helped to change all that. It has created a focal point: a place where any birdwatcher, however inexperienced, can chat to other enthusiasts, get advice, and above all 'have a go'. Every year now, I meet people who've just taken up watching birds, yet who can come along to the fair and rub shoulders with experts such as Ian Wallace, Bruce Pearson and Bill Oddie, getting the benefit of their vast knowledge and experience.

It's great for children, too. This year I'm taking along my son James, who has heard about the fair's delights from his big brother David, and now wants to see for himself. Where else could you let an eight-year-old child wander around on his own, enjoying his freedom without the risk of danger? And where else can a child spend three whole days and still not say 'Daddy, I'm bored!'

New Year in Sussex

 JANUARY 1999

New Year's Day is traditionally a time for renewal: for seeing the familiar, day-to-day world through new eyes. For birdwatchers, things are no different. We drag ourselves out of bed on the morning of 1 January, shake off the hangover from the night before, and head out to start our 'year list'. The aim: to see as many different species as possible between the hours of dawn and dusk.

That, at least, is the theory. Unfortunately the dawn start didn't quite go as planned, and it was just before nine when Suzanne and I began the drive down to Pagham Harbour in Sussex. Pagham is one of my favourite birding sites. It has great scenery, a wide variety of habitats and a good range of birds, with the potential for surprises.

Despite the recent run of wet and windy weather, conditions were sunny and warm, with blue skies and a brisk southerly breeze. The tide at Pagham village was higher than I'd ever seen it, lapping against the base of the sea wall, and forcing the birds to seek refuge in nearby fields.

Thousands of Golden Plovers and Lapwings were wheeling overhead, filling the sky as they twisted and turned, constantly calling to each other in a breathtaking spectacle. Hundreds of ducks were on the open water: mainly Wigeon, Teal and Pintails. There was also a lone, smaller bird, whose black-and-white plumage reminded me of an auk. It was a Slavonian Grebe, one of Pagham's winter specialities. Then an elegant white bird flew past: a Little Egret, once very rare, but now a regular sight on many south-coast estuaries.

After a brisk walk, we drove round to the other side of the harbour, where the car park at Church Norton was filling up with birders, dog-walkers and worshippers at the little church that gives the village its name. As the tide rose to new heights, thousands of waders flocked together, flashing light and dark as their plumage caught the winter sun. But the real prize was away from the harbour, by the little gate at the entrance to the churchyard. Here, a small crowd of birders had gathered, watching an ivy-covered tree with more intensity than it appeared to deserve.

Then a tiny bird popped out, revealing a stunning black-and-white striped head, fiery orange crown and olive-green plumage, before plunging back into the dense foliage. It was a Firecrest, a rare relative of the Goldcrest, and just as small – 9cm long and weighing barely the same as a 20p coin. After a few frustratingly brief glimpses, the bird, which is spending the winter in this sheltered, balmy place, finally revealed itself in all its miniature glory, much to everyone's relief and delight.

On leaving Pagham, the day's total stood at a respectable 58 species. To boost it further, we stopped off on the way home, at the RSPB's Pulborough Brooks reserve. As well as the attractions of a well-stocked shop and superb tearoom, Pulborough is a magnet for wintering birds, with large numbers of dabbling ducks on the flood plain and flocks of Redwings in the fields above.

The hide was so full we could barely get a seat. We soon found out why. A Barn Owl was quartering the marshes, hovering on its broad, pale wings in search of voles. After a few near-misses, it finally caught one, only for an opportunistic Kestrel to make a smash-and-grab raid and seize the prey. Bewildered, the owl flew up to perch on a fence-post, treating us all to a splendid view as we sympathised with its misfortune.

As we walked back up the muddy path to a well-earned cup of tea, the day's final total stood at 65 species. But mere numbers tell nothing. Three very different images will stay in my memory: the Barn Owl floating on silent wings, flocks of Golden Plovers wheeling overhead in the pale blue sky, and that tiny jewel of a bird, the Firecrest. Happy New Year!

The unforgettable Farnes

 AUGUST 1999

As a spotty teenager, I remember listening to the Newcastle-based band Lindisfarne. It wasn't for another 20 years or so that I finally visited the stretch of Northumberland coast from which the band took their name. Since then, I've gone back as often as I can: lured by the cries of nesting seabirds on the Farne Islands nearby. Mind you, the racket made by several thousand Kittiwakes, auks and terns can easily outdo most rock bands. It starts as a distant hum, then, as the boat approaches the rocky cliffs, builds to a crescendo until the noise is almost deafening.

Then there's the indescribable smell. In other parts of the world, seabird droppings, or guano, are harvested for fuel, bringing riches to the residents. Here, though, the only people making money are the local boatmen, whose canny monopoly allows them to charge a tidy sum for putting you off on Staple Island, picking you up a couple of hours later, then depositing you on Inner Farne.

Still, it's worth every penny. There are very few places where I've been so overwhelmed by the sheer presence of living creatures. Grey Seals loll on the rocks, supremely indifferent to the passing boat. Common, Arctic and Sandwich Terns swoop overhead, plunging down into the water to pick up their prey. And Guillemots and Razorbills – truly the penguins of the north – perch like statues on the cliff face above the boat.

Then there's the one we've all come to see: the Puffin. This comical black-and-white auk, with its multicoloured bill, must surely rival the Robin as Britain's favourite bird. In late July there are literally thousands of them, hanging about outside their burrows as if challenging the photographer to come up with an image which isn't yet another tired cliché. Hundreds of rolls of film must be exposed here every year, all to produce more or less the same image – yet this knowledge still didn't stop me taking a few dozen photos myself.

But despite the teeming birdlife and golden photo opportunities, all is not well on the Farne Islands. Although we searched diligently through the flocks on the beach, we couldn't find any Arctic Tern chicks. One of the National Trust wardens explained why. Apparently it has been a disastrous breeding season, with the parents unable to find enough food for their hungry young. As a result, 200 pairs of Arctic Terns have only managed to raise a single chick between them.

Nobody knows why it's been such a bad year for the terns. It may be that pollution on the surface of the sea has forced their prey – sand eels – to venture deeper than usual, out of the birds' reach. Maybe overfishing is to blame. Or perhaps rising sea temperatures, due to global warming, have reduced the numbers of fish in the area altogether. Whatever the reason, in a month's time 400 Arctic Terns will be making the long flight south to Antarctica – without their offspring.

Fortunately, other birds are having a more successful breeding season. Baby Shags, looking like fluffy children's toys, savoured the regurgitated food served up by their parents. Kittiwake chicks perched on ledges, looking as if they were about to fall off at any moment. And the Puffins continued to loaf about, posing for photographs until the boat finally came to take us away.

Back on shore, it almost seemed like a dream. But that evening, on the beach by Bamburgh Castle, we looked over the narrow stretch of sea to the Farne Islands. In the air, above the distant rocks, there was a mass of wheeling seabirds. All that was missing was the sound – and, of course, that unforgettable smell . . .

Precious ivory

 JANUARY 2000

Few birds on the British list have quite the same air of mystery about them as the Ivory Gull. This is a bird of the true Arctic: breeding among the pack-ice of Spitzbergen and Novaya Zemlya, and surviving by scavenging the remains of Polar Bear kills. Even in the long, dark winter it rarely ventures south of the Arctic Ocean.

So when I heard the news that an Ivory Gull had taken up residence in the Suffolk seaside town of Aldeburgh, my reaction was a mixture of astonishment and glee. The bird had probably followed a fishing trawler south from the Arctic Ocean, and was now spending its time on the beach, feeding on scraps donated by friendly local fishermen.

On a visit to East Anglia the weekend before Christmas, we decided to drop in on the bird. As we arrived, a small group of birders stood with their telescopes pointing up at the roof of a building. It was the usual story. Apparently the gull had been 'showing well' a minute or so before we got there, but had just flown away.

So in the gathering gloom of a winter's afternoon, we braved the bitter northerly wind and strode along the beach. At first, there were only Black-headed, Herring and Great Black-backed Gulls, but then I caught sight of a blinding flash of white. We walked around the corner of a fisherman's hut, and there it was: my first ever sighting of an Ivory Gull.

Despite its name, this species is not ivory coloured at all. A better name might be 'Persil Gull': its plumage is almost whiter than white, apart from dark legs, a pinkish bill, and little black spots along the wings and tail. At first sight, with its suitably funny walk, it looked more like some exotic pigeon than a gull. Its pristine appearance was marred by what can only be described as a dirty face, the result of a life spent sticking its head inside a carcass in order to feed.

Living in the high Arctic, birds face a simple choice: eat or die. This bird had decided to eat, attacking a dead fish with gusto, while the accompanying Black-headed Gulls simply looked on bemused. If one did attempt to muscle in on the new arrival's territory it got pretty short shrift from the Ivory Gull.

As we stood and watched, I became aware of the incongruity of the situation. Here we were, standing around on a Sunday afternoon in a genteel English seaside resort, watching a bird which until recently had never even seen a human being. From time to time curious passers-by stopped and asked what we were doing, then took a look through our telescopes, made non-committal remarks and wandered off. I imagined them returning to their homes and greeting their spouses with: 'You'll never guess what I saw down on the beach, dear . . .'

For me, however, seeing this bird fulfilled a long-held ambition. I first became aware of the Ivory Gull in the early 1970s, when one turned up unexpectedly somewhere in north-east England, prompting one of the first examples of a 'mass twitch'. Since then, I had always wanted to see one, and now the bird was making short work of a fish just a few metres in front of me. It appeared to be very much at home in the freezing conditions.

With dusk rapidly advancing, I only had one remaining desire: to see this ethereal wanderer in flight. My wish was granted, as the gull took off and floated around our heads, uttering a surprisingly high-pitched cry. As it dropped down onto the beach to roost, the first flakes of snow began to fall.

Forty years on

 MAY 2000

Coming just a few days after my fortieth birthday, the first May Day of the new millennium seemed like a good time to revisit an old haunt – Stodmarsh in Kent. The aim was to reacquaint ourselves with a host of summer visitors, newly returned from Africa. We decided to make a day of it, so seven adults and four children met up to walk across the reserve, in the Stour Valley just east of Canterbury. Our ultimate destination was Grove Ferry, where a pint of local ale and a pub lunch awaited us.

At first, things didn't look too promising. Mist, low temperatures and a biting wind conspired to keep the birds out of sight, so although we could hear several species singing, there was not a lot to see. The first hide produced very little apart from distant Common Terns, Mallards and a few Great Crested Grebes. Outside, as the mist began to lift, we saw our first Whitethroat and Reed Bunting, typical inhabitants of the reedbed and its surrounding scrub.

As we wandered along the path the children soon lost interest in birds and began to play traditional games, such as Pokemon, hitting each other with sticks and jumping in muddy puddles. We stuck to our guns, however, and were rewarded with stunning views of a singing male Sedge Warbler, two Reed Warblers fighting (and almost drowning in the process) and a glimpse of Stodmarsh's loudest inhabitant, Cetti's Warbler. An even more elusive resident, a Water Rail, squealed like a stuck pig but never revealed itself.

After about a mile the path becomes more wooded. Almost immediately, we heard a rapid, tuneful phrase, uttered by a Garden Warbler. Easily overlooked, this is one of the most nondescript of all our warblers, with no diagnostic features apart from its beady, black eye. Fortunately my partner Suzanne caught a glimpse of the bird to confirm its identity. By the time we reached the other end of the footpath our stomachs were rumbling, though a Willow Warbler still managed to make itself heard above the din. Seven species of warbler by lunchtime – not bad!

After lunch, we took the alternative route back, through the new English Nature reserve at Grove Ferry. This already has an excellent reputation among birders, and it certainly lived up to expectations. By now the sun was out, along with thousands of Sand Martins, hawking for insects while uttering their trilling call. Some came so close we could almost feel the air from their wingbeats as they passed. Then, out of nowhere, came the bird we were hoping to see: a Hobby, scything through the sky like a giant Swift. It was soon joined by several others, and we watched as they grabbed insects in midair, barely interrupting their progress as they passed food from claws to beak in one flowing movement.

More migrants appeared: Yellow Wagtails looking like flying lemons, little flocks of Swifts, and an elegant Greenshank feeding in a flooded field. Our entrance to the next hide was blocked by a quagmire, and we considered giving it a miss. Fortunately one of our party was wearing wellies and was willing to trudge through the mud. Almost immediately he beckoned us inside. To our delight there was a Common Crane feeding only a short distance away. This bird had been around the Stour Valley for a week or two, but was nevertheless an unexpected treat. Even my son James was impressed.

As the afternoon heat sapped our strength, we strolled back to the car park, pausing only to listen to a Blackcap in full song, our eighth and final species of warbler for the day. A day in which we had seen some wonderful birds, had a lovely walk, enjoyed a pub lunch and, most importantly of all, tired out the kids.

Perfect day

 FEBRUARY 2001

There are some days that make you realise why you took up bird-watching in the first place. The last Sunday in January was one of them. It wasn't the scenery that made it so memorable: we spent the day around Dungeness, whose views – dominated by shingle and the nuclear power stations – are something of an acquired taste. In the end, it was a combination of good company, great birds, lovely weather and the freshest fish and chips in Kent, at the Pilot Inn.

We didn't even start until nine, after a leisurely breakfast with our friends Nigel and Cheryle, at their cottage in Sussex. Toast and mar-malade were accompanied by close-up views of a Nuthatch and Marsh Tit, regular visitors to their birdtable.

Once we got going, our first stop was a gravel-pit near Rye, to look for a rare Ferruginous Duck. It proved elusive, but we enjoyed four Smew in compensation. A few miles further on, we reached Scotney Gravel Pits, home to huge numbers of Wigeon and Pochard, and thou-sands of gulls. We had just poured some coffee when Suzanne noticed a large, grey bird heading low over the water. It was a young Peregrine, causing panic among the ducks. Peregrines are always a fine bird to see, and this one seemed to bring us luck. Nigel immediately spotted a Black-necked Grebe among the dabchicks, and we finished our coffee in excellent spirits.

A few miles further on, we reached the coast, where we took a short walk across the shingle to Lade Gravel Pits. We failed to see the drake Canvasback, a rare North American duck which has taken up semi-permanent residence. But we did see a Kittiwake, at least a dozen Smew, including five splendid males, and a Dartford Warbler. This little bird kept popping up in the gorse bushes right in front of us, giving superb views.

Indeed, it was a day of excellent views, due to fabulous light and

Nigel's powerful new telescope. We enjoyed the Smew; a cracking Slavonian Grebe, seen from the comfort of the RSPB visitor centre; and a flock of 50 White-fronted Geese among their feral Canada and Greylag cousins on Denge Marsh.

By now it was mid-afternoon, and time to head west for an evening spectacle that promised to top off the day. On the way, I tuned into Radio Five Live to hear that West Ham, the team I have supported almost as long as I have been birding, were leading 1-0 against the mighty Manchester United in the FA Cup.

Now I faced a dilemma. We had arrived at Rye Harbour, and my companions were eager to get going. I pleaded with them to wait until the match was over, to which they reluctantly agreed. Five minutes later, we headed down the path to join a small crowd of people. The story was a familiar one: 'You should have been here five minutes ago – a Bittern flew right into the reedbed!' As you can imagine, I was not the most popular member of our party.

Fortunately, things soon began to look up. First, a distant Barn Owl quartered the marsh, and two Kingfishers flew up and down in front of us. Then, a dozen Little Egrets came in to roost in the trees. Finally, to my great relief, two Bitterns flew in low, then plunged down into the reedbed, before one reappeared for a brief encore. As the sun set, even the sky turned claret and blue. Perhaps God is a West Ham fan after all.

Dragons and damsels

JULY 2001

Wicken Fen is not only Britain's oldest nature reserve, but also one of its very best. An oasis of wildlife in the agricultural desert of Cambridgeshire, it boasts a greater variety of creatures than almost anywhere else in the country. On a week's visit earlier this month I enjoyed views of Woodcocks and Hobbies, Marsh Harriers and Reed

Buntings. But although Wicken is excellent for birds, it was the other wildlife that really caught my eye: especially the smaller creatures. And of all the beetles, bees, bugs and other insects I saw, by far the most fascinating were the dragonflies.

Until now, I have barely given dragonflies a second glance. I have occasionally noticed them as they cruise up and down on sunny days, and enjoy watching the delicate blue damselflies (though I must admit that for years I thought they were called mayflies). Last year I got to know one or two of the commoner species, including the Four-spotted Chaser, which confusingly has two spots on each of its four wings, making eight in all; and the Emperor, which, at four inches long with a whopping six-inch wingspan, is the biggest insect you are ever likely to see in Britain.

My visit to Wicken really opened my eyes to these beautiful creatures. I saw at least 15 different species and, with a little help from an excellent new field guide, even managed to identify most of them for myself. Just like birds, dragonflies have their own 'jizz', that indefinable quality that enables you to tell them apart even on brief views. So Emperors cruise along as if surveying their kingdom, while the Brown Hawker flies up and down constantly but hardly ever lands. In flight, jizz is the best way to identify most species, but when they land you can get great views, especially with modern close-focusing binoculars.

During my stay I learnt to distinguish between Ruddy and Common Darters, looking for the pinched abdomen of the former, and to tell Black-tailed Skimmer by its fat blue body with a black tip. Red-eyed Damselfly was dead easy, as its name suggests, while Large Red and Blue-tailed Damselflies were not too hard to pick out. But when it came to identifying three very similar damselflies – the Common Blue, Azure and Variable – I lost my patience. Checking each segment of their bodies for diagnostic markings was not my idea of fun, so I gave up and let the experts point them out.

But one damselfly really did stand out from the crowd. Along one of the 'lodes' – narrow drainage ditches – I came across several

Banded Demoiselles, an absolutely stunning little insect with a dark green body and bright blue bands on its wings. How I have failed to see these gorgeous creatures in the past I just don't know.

So on sunny days for the next month or two, I shall be venturing to dragonfly hotspots such as the Wetland Centre in Barnes and Thursley Common in Surrey to search for dragons and damsels. And if by setting my binoculars to permanent close focus I miss some of the birds flying over my head, so be it. Now that I have discovered this new and magical world, I can't wait to explore it.

In search of the Corncrake

 AUGUST 2001

I first visited the Outer Hebrides in the mid-1980s, on a cycling holiday with my best mate Rob. We took the low road along the western side of the islands, as opposed to the more hilly eastern side – our excuse being that in those days we didn't have mountain bikes, and so had to stick to the tarmac.

My abiding memory of the trip is of the grating sound which assaulted our ears every morning, noon and night – a repetitive noise which has been compared to the sound of a steel comb being drawn across a piece of wood. It came from a small bird, about the size and shape of a Moorhen, whose scientific name, *Crex crex*, derives from its bizarre call. Known by the poet John Clare as the Landrail, these days its common name is the Corncrake.

Corncrakes are the Scarlet Pimpernel of the bird world. You seek them here, you seek them there, you seek those damned Corncrakes everywhere. But you never actually see them. I remember standing and staring at patches of vegetation for hours on end, willing the noisy bird to appear, even for a brief moment – just so I could say I had seen it.

It never did. I had to wait another six years before I finally saw a Corncrake, at the RSPB reserve at Balranald on North Uist. Even then it was hardly what you would call a classic view. Just a small, rat-like creature scurrying along the edge of a field, then disappearing from sight.

So when I returned to North Uist with a film crew earlier this year I was not all that confident. Sure, I had been told that a particularly obliging bird was performing to all and sundry – virtually dancing a jig on top of some rocks, according to one observer. It had even been filmed by one of my colleagues, who gleefully rang me up to tell me of his triumph.

Of course, when we turned up the bird had a sudden attack of stage fright, and although it continued to deliver its incessant craking call, it would not show itself, on camera or otherwise. Things were not helped by the strengthening breeze, or the fact that the vegetation in the field was even longer than usual thanks to a warm, sunny spring.

After a while, when you listen to a Corncrake you go into a kind of Zen-like trance. Every now and then there was a little movement – the bird or just a gust of wind blowing the grass? As I stood and waited, I recalled Clare's wonderful description of the bird as 'a sort of living doubt'. Was I the victim of an overactive imagination? Did the bird exist at all? Should we just give up and go home?

And then it appeared. First a beak, then the whole head, a quick look left and right, and a scurry – and it had gone. We held our breath, waiting for the bird to show itself again, but in vain. We turned to John, our cameraman, and I raised my eyebrow in beseeching enquiry. He nodded and smiled. Not exactly a classic portrait, but as we later agreed, 'a birder's view' – one that would be instantly familiar to anyone who has ever looked for this frustrating and elusive bird.

Journey to St Kilda

 AUGUST 2002

We set sail from the Scottish port of Oban in bright, warm sunshine. The sea was not quite as smooth as a millpond, but certainly calm enough to suggest an easy voyage to come. Our destination was the island group of St Kilda – the remotest, wildest, and most inaccessible place in Britain.

Some 50 miles or so to the north-west of the Outer Hebrides, St Kilda is best-known for being home to what naturalist Sir Julian Huxley called 'the bird people'. They lived there for centuries, harvesting the seabirds, until they were finally evacuated in 1930. Since then, apart from visiting scientists and contractors, the islands have remained uninhabited.

On our voyage, although the sunny weather lasted, the calm, flat seas did not. Next day, our yacht *Silurian* hit the Minch, and the Minch hit back. Winds forecast at force four to five turned out to be force five to six, gusting force seven. The seas rose and fell, and the boat pitched and rolled with them – already our goal of filming on St Kilda was looking doubtful. Things became even worse when, mid-morning, presenter Bill Oddie emerged from his cabin, muttered a few well-chosen oaths against the sea, his producer and life itself, and returned groaning to his bed.

Meanwhile I was beginning to feel a little green myself, so to counter the boat's roller-coaster motion I stared firmly at the horizon. Five minutes later, what looked like a giant sardine shot out of the water, hung briefly in mid-air, and crashed back beneath the waves. 'Whale!' was the only possible response. And indeed it was: a young Minke Whale, breaching into the air in what looked like pure enjoyment.

Both boat and camera crews mobilised immediately: the former recording details of the sighting for the Hebridean Whale and Dolphin

Trust; the latter capturing the moment on video. Three more jumps, and the whale disappeared beneath the waves for the last time. It was a great cure for seasickness.

But a couple of hours later, things really took a turn for the worse. I awoke from a nap to discover that, because of rough weather, we had diverted eastwards to the Isle of Skye. As Bill so succinctly put it: 'Twenty-four hours sailing and we're still on the flippin' mainland!'

More to the point, we were still at least a day's sailing from our destination. After a good night's sleep, we held a summit meeting to discuss the contingency plan, which involved cutting short our trip and pottering around the Inner Hebrides instead. At this point, our skipper Alan intervened. In a calm, measured Irish brogue he pointed out that the weather forecast was improving, the seas were calming down, and we had a real chance to fulfil our quest. Like Cortez's men, we stared at each other with a wild surmise, and made the decision: we would give it a go.

The journey across to North Uist was uneventful, the Sound of Harris calm, and the weather perfect. After dinner, we retired to our cabins, leaving the crew to sail through the night in shifts. I awoke at 5 a.m., struggled out on deck and found myself enveloped in dense mist. According to the ship's instruments we were only a mile or two from our destination, but all I could see was the bow of the boat. I was reminded of the pioneering explorer Martin Martin, who in 1697 sailed right past St Kilda before realising his mistake, and turning round just in time.

Then, as I stared into the fog, it appeared. A vast, grey cliff face, and thousands of swirling seabirds, looming out of the mist above me. After 60 hours sailing, we had finally arrived at the fabled islands of St Kilda. The journey was over, and the real adventure was about to begin.

St Kilda: fantasy island

 SEPTEMBER 2002

It had always been my ambition to visit St Kilda – surely the most inaccessible and wildest place in Britain. So when, after two and a half days sailing, we finally arrived, I was prepared for disappointment – surely the reality could not live up to my imagination. But I was wrong. St Kilda really is the most incredible place I have ever been.

As our yacht dropped anchor in Village Bay, the fog cleared, and Kilda revealed itself at last – vast cliffs and rocky stacks looming over our tiny boat. And there, high on the hillside overlooking the bay, I saw the legacy of its former inhabitants.

For hundreds, possibly thousands of years until their final evacuation in 1930, the islanders lived almost entirely on seabirds: Gannets, Fulmars and Puffins. Having captured them by scaling the cliffs and clambering up steep stacks, they dried them in stone cairns known as 'cleits'. Today, these massive structures are one of the most striking features of the St Kilda landscape – a Scottish version of the famous Easter Island statues.

Our first day on the island turned unexpectedly fine and sunny. We lost no time in filming the scenery and its wildlife: even getting attacked by a pair of Arctic Skuas, which also harassed one of the island's three specialities, the Soay sheep. Lower down, the cleits and dry stone walls are host to St Kilda's two other unique creatures: the island races of the wren and field mouse. Both are larger than their mainland cousins, and the wren is noticeably darker and greyer. The wrens live up to their scientific name of 'troglodytes', nesting in cracks and crevices. The field mice prefer the houses, emerging at dusk each evening to search the path for morsels of food.

Later on, as I walked along 'Main Street' at dusk, I felt as though I was walking back in time. It may be over 70 years since the people of

St Kilda finally abandoned the island, but at times like this it can almost feel as if they have left their ghosts behind.

I tried to imagine what it must have been like to have lived, as generations of islanders did, on the very edge of the world. What did they think when cruise ships full of sightseeing Victorians came sailing into their little harbour? Did they resent being the objects of tourist curiosity, much as a remote tribe in the Amazon rainforest might do today? And how did they feel as they boarded the evacuation boat in August 1930, and left their home behind for the very last time?

Next morning, we set sail for home. As we left, I stared at the retreating landmass until it finally vanished into the mist. I felt mixed emotions: a sense of awe, privilege and wonder, as well as sadness that I may never see St Kilda again. But even if I never go back, I will always have the memories of visiting one of the most incredible places, not just in Britain, but in the world.

New Year in Norfolk

 JANUARY 2003

The New Year saw us back in one of our favourite haunts, north Norfolk, with three whole days to enjoy its many delights. Apart from fine pub food and the county's magnificent churches, these included exactly 100 species of bird – not bad for the middle of winter.

On the very first afternoon, I confess that I broke my 'no twitching' rule. The bird in question was a Pallid Harrier, and although I have watched these in their more usual surroundings of Israel's Negev Desert, I decided that any bird this far away from home deserved the courtesy of a visit. Unfortunately, after we had tramped along a muddy track and joined several dozen nervous twitchers, the bird itself failed to appear. As the mist closed in and dusk fell, we retreated to the comforts of a local hostelry for a meal the size of a small horse, though considerably more tasty.

Next morning dawned cold and wet, but we headed off in high spirits. First stop was the RSPB reserve at Strumpshaw Fen just east of Norwich, where after a slow start we caught a glimpse of Britain's loudest songbird, Cetti's Warbler. Great views of Marsh Harriers were followed by the discovery of a flock of Siskins, among which two Bullfinches were an unexpected and welcome sight.

In some years, hundreds of Waxwings visit our shores in search of winter food, but this year there must be plenty of berries in Scandinavia, because only a single bird has been reported. Rather foolishly, we attempted to find it, following precise instructions from Birdline East Anglia, which directed us to the nearest bush. Or at least they would have, had I not misheard them. So after a consolatory cup of coffee we headed off to the Broads, in search of easier birds to see.

And we found them. A Barn Owl, performing beautifully just outside the village of Hickling; at least a dozen Marsh Harriers, and two or three Hen Harriers, coming into roost at nearby Stubb Mill; and the pièce de résistance, three cranes flying overhead in the gathering gloom.

On Saturday, we followed the well-trodden path of the north coast, the highlight being a flock of 50 Shore Larks in a blizzard on Holkham Beach. Another try for the Pallid Harrier produced distant and deeply unsatisfying views, and the spectacle of mass doubt among the gathering hordes of twitchers – could they count it or not? Dinner with friends at the George in Cley fortified us for our final morning at Titchwell, though a diversion to see several thousand Pink-footed Geese feeding in a beet field meant that our first priority on arrival was lunch. Our hunger satisfied, we enjoyed close-up views of a variety of waders, including Snipe, Spotted Redshank and the resident Black-winged Stilt (rumoured to be an escape from a nearby bird collection), before being drawn back to the pleasures of the reserve's café.

So, a stone or two heavier, we headed home, suitably relaxed and prepared to return to work on Monday morning. By the time I reached Bristol, Norfolk – and its pubs, churches and wonderful birds – seemed a million miles away. It took a solitary Blackcap, gorging itself on mimosa berries outside the BBC canteen, to remind me that you can enjoy watching birds almost anywhere.

Heaven in Devon

 FEBRUARY 2004

If you want to see lots of different birds in winter, you could do a lot worse than head down to Devon. A mild climate, a range of habitats and plenty of food attract large numbers of wintering birds, most of which are pretty easy to see.

A great place to start is Bowling Green Marsh, by the River Exe at Topsham. I have a soft spot for this little riverside town, as my grandmother was born and brought up there, so it was good to sit in the plush RSPB hide and watch the action. As it was still low tide, this mainly consisted of ducks such as Wigeon, Teal and Pintails – some already displaying to each other in the first week of February. Two unexpected bonuses were a Spoonbill, and the even rarer Glossy Ibis, both of which have been here for some time now, to the delight of local birders.

For another local speciality, Cirl Bunting, we headed down to a National Trust farm south of Brixham. Conservation work and a return to traditional farming methods have brought this species back from the brink of extinction as a British breeding bird, and we saw at least half a dozen, including some splendid males. It seemed fitting to be watching Cirl Buntings so close to the home of the man who first found them in Britain, the nineteenth-century ornithologist George Montagu.

You can't go to Devon without visiting the seaside – even in February! A walk along the beach at Broadsands produced several Mediterranean Gulls, as well as a motley collection of birds on the sea, including Razorbills and a Black-necked Grebe.

Away from the coast, we dropped in on some friends, who have moved down from London to a splendid Edwardian house surrounded by woods and paddocks, on the edge of Dartmoor. Their garden produced a wonderful free show: Blue, Great and Coal Tits; a Nuthatch and Treecreeper; and dozens of Chaffinches and House Sparrows – all coming to the well-stocked feeders. Seven-year-old twins Donald and Hattie eagerly pointed out the different species, and I was able to add Marsh Tit to their burgeoning 'garden list'.

For an unexpected spectacle, we visited the unlikely location of a pedestrianised shopping precinct in the town of Newton Abbot. Just as the shops closed, and people headed home, we could hear the sound of birds calling to each other in the sky above. At first they seemed reluctant to come down; then one or two landed on the shop roofs, confirming their identity as Pied Wagtails. As dusk fell, dozens of them plunged down into a couple of trees outside Marks & Spencer's, where they spend the night huddling up against each other for warmth, safe from any predators beneath the neon lights. With at least 400 individuals, it was like a benevolent version of Hitchcock's *The Birds*.

The experience was a timely reminder of the true wonder of birding. For no matter how long you have been watching birds and how many rare vagrants you see, the real thrill comes from seeing a common and familiar species in an unexpected setting. So next time you're wandering through a shopping centre at dusk, listen out for the telltale sounds of a wagtail roost.

Wild in Wiltshire

 AUGUST 2004

One of the great advantages of birdwatching – compared with most other forms of watching wildlife – is that there is always something to see, no matter what the time of year. Nevertheless, there are still quiet months, and August can be one of them, especially away from the coast.

Fortunately, August is a great time to check out other flying creatures, such as butterflies, moths, dragonflies and damselflies. And for the birder who wants to extend his or her horizons, watching butterflies or dragonflies is a good place to start. There are about 60 different kinds of butterfly breeding in Britain, and fewer than 40 different dragonflies, so it's not too daunting – especially if, like me, you have spent most of your life ignoring anything that doesn't have a full set of feathers.

Recently I've spent some time in Wiltshire, one of the best counties in Britain for a wide range of flying insects. Sunny mornings and afternoons are the best time for 'dragons and damsels', and fortunately my visits coincided with fine weather. At Cotswold Water Park almost every piece of vegetation was festooned with Common Blue Damselflies, their bodies glowing in the sunshine. Nearby, larger dragonflies such as Emperors, Southern Hawkers and Brown Hawkers cruised up and down, patrolling their territory like First World War biplanes. All three are easy to identify: the Emperor has a bright blue abdomen, while that of the Southern Hawker is emerald green. The Brown Hawker lives up to its name: not only is its body brown, but the wings are a sort of yellowish buff.

But this summer, for me at least, the butterflies have been the real stars of the show. Like most people, I've always been able to identify obvious ones such as Red Admiral, Peacock and Small Tortoiseshell; and over the past few years I've made an effort to learn other common species such as Meadow Brown and Gatekeeper. But this is the first time I've gone in search of more specialised butterflies: in this case, those found on the chalk downlands of southern England.

I started off by learning to identify the most obvious kinds, such as the exquisite Small Copper, and the striking Marbled White. Then, as I gained in confidence, I managed to tick off Common Blue, Ringlet and Brown Argus – the latter with the help of my colleague Mike, who is a real expert at butterfly identification.

Then, as we searched the ramparts of the Iron Age fort at Barbury Castle, I had a moment of pure beginner's luck. Scanning through my binoculars, I caught sight of a butterfly with strikingly pale underwings, marked with a scattering of spots. As it opened up, revealing delicate, pale powder-blue upperwings, I heard myself call out 'Chalkhill Blue!' Fortunately my instant identification was correct, and for the next hour or so we watched these beautiful insects as they fluttered back and forth to feed.

In that moment, I remembered what it was like to be a novice birder again: to see a special bird for the very first time and, by a combination of luck and judgement, to put a name to it. Now I'm well and truly hooked, and can't wait until next spring, when I shall go in search of more beautiful British butterflies.

Big winter's day

 FEBRUARY 2005

As regular readers of this column will know, sometime in early January I usually try to devote a whole day to go out and enjoy our local birds. True to form, this year I took a jaunt around west London, enjoying the scenic beauty of its gravel-pits, reservoirs and other man-made bird haunts. As always, I was accompanied by my birding buddy Neil, whose laid-back attitude fortunately matches my own.

Neil and I do not favour the dawn starts on which many keen birders insist. Indeed, the sun was well up when we set off from my home in Hampton, heading towards our first location, the ornamental lake at Virginia Water. On the way we ticked off the usual suspects: various gulls, pigeons and crows, though not, as yet, any House Sparrows.

Despite the mild weather, Virginia Water was more than usually productive. Its local speciality, the stunning Mandarin Duck, proved surprisingly easy; while in the woods we saw Nuthatches, Siskins, Redpolls and Goldcrests. Little flocks of Redwings flew overhead, a constant feature of the day in a winter when these charming Scandinavian thrushes seem to be everywhere. We did, however, miss out on Treecreepers; just one of several species we never quite managed to catch up with during the day.

By mid-morning, we had reached one of my childhood haunts, Wraysbury Gravel Pits. There, we bagged the winter duck trio of Goldeneye, Goosander and Smew, before moving swiftly on to another location from my youth, Staines Reservoirs. There we really noticed the mildness of the weather: normally a visit to Staines requires at least ten layers of clothing, but we hardly needed a coat. The birds still performed, however, and by the time we left, just before one o'clock, we had seen a total of 57 species.

From this point it often becomes difficult to add new birds to the list, so we decided to go for the big one – a flock of a rare northern invader reported near Bracknell. Our directions were sketchy, so we wasted half an hour driving around the outskirts of the town, before we finally caught sight of a flock of Starling-shaped birds on the edge of a housing estate. Fortunately they were not Starlings, but Waxwings – another bird which has arrived in large numbers this winter, gorging themselves on berries in suburban locations throughout Britain.

We saw an unexpected Buzzard on our way back along the M3; while an hour at the London Wetland Centre in Barnes brought a

Water Rail and Snipe – the latter spotted by an eight-year-old girl, much to the chagrin of the assembled birders.

By now, we were still missing one bird we used to take for granted: the humble House Sparrow. Just as we had almost given up, as we stopped at traffic lights in Teddington we heard a familiar chirp: sparrow finally ticked off. As the light faded, a rapid visit to Bushy Park gave us Egyptian Goose and the roosting Tawny Owls, together with spectacular fly-pasts of Ring-necked Parakeets on their way to roost.

We added the 70th and final bird of the day, Yellow-legged Gull, in almost total darkness at Hampton filter beds. A short drive home for a welcome cuppa, and a quick discussion of what we missed – Sparrowhawk, Grey Wagtail and that elusive Treecreeper. Still, there's always next year . . .

CHAPTER 5

Birding abroad

1994–2005

I had reached the age of 29, and had been watching birds for more than a quarter of a century, before I finally did any serious birding abroad. The occasion was a 'birding package holiday' to Israel run by the tour group Sunbird, and it blew my mind. At the end of a week I had not only seen close to 200 species, a third of which were 'lifers'. I had also reinvigorated my passion for birds.

Another, even more crucial event occurred on that trip. Having spent two hectic days in the Negev Desert with the legendary Israeli birder Hadoram Shirihai, I offered to write an account of the trip for the magazine *Birding World*. This duly appeared in print, and my career as a writer on all things ornithological had finally begun.

Since that first trip, I have travelled to six of the world's seven continents in search of birds. Many of these trips were courtesy of the

BBC licence-payer and accompanied by a film crew: I have been with Bill Oddie to Florida, Trinidad & Tobago, Israel, Mallorca, Poland, the Netherlands, New Jersey, Iceland, California and Patagonia; with Michaela Strachan to Antarctica; and with the *Big Cat Diary* team to the Masai Mara. Others were simply for pleasure, including our honeymoon to The Gambia.

What they all have in common – apart, of course, from the birds – are the people we met, who helped us in our travels, many of whom have become lifelong friends. This chapter is dedicated to them.

Summer in the Vendée

 JULY 1994

You have to get up pretty early in the morning to beat a Black Kite to its breakfast. Unlike most birds of prey, which wait until later in the day before taking to the air on rising thermals, kites launch themselves on their long, narrow wings well before sunrise. At this time of day, they have the place to themselves, which may explain why the Black Kite is the world's commonest and, arguably, most successful raptor.

But not in Britain – not yet, anyway. These daybreak hunters were a few hundred miles to the south, in the Vendée region of western France. To the English eye, the place seems strangely familiar – indeed you could almost be in Sussex, if it weren't for the weather. For during the summer months, the Vendée enjoys blue skies and sunshine, broken only by the occasional thunderstorm. As a result, the mean July temperature is a couple of degrees higher than southern Britain.

The region's birdlife reflects this warmer climate. As well as the ever-present kites, there is at least one Little Egret in every pool – a bright, white apparition stalking its underwater prey. And every patch of trees seems to hold a singing Serin – a smaller relative of the domestic canary, whose song sounds like a bunch of jangling keys.

Among the grazing cattle on the marshes south of the medieval walled city of Brouage, I discovered a wealth of birds: Purple Herons, Marsh Harriers and dazzling Blue-headed Wagtails on every fence-post. My ears were assaulted by the repetitive, jangling song of the Great Reed Warbler, which looks and sounds like a common-or-garden Reed Warbler on steroids. Almost the size of a thrush, it clings onto the bending reed-stems for dear life, while belting out its extraordinary song from a bright orange gape.

Nearby, I came across a magnificent White Stork, knee-deep in the marsh, searching for its amphibian quarry. A few pairs of these statuesque birds breed here, on specially provided nesting platforms. Further along, a bird by the roadside proved to be a Cattle Egret. This species is currently spreading north at a rapid pace, and if events elsewhere in the world are anything to go by, might colonise Britain within a decade or two.

And it may not be alone. If the latest predictions on global warming come true, and Britain experiences temperature rises of between one and two degrees Celsius by the middle of the twenty-first century, then many species currently found along the Atlantic coasts of France may find the more sheltered parts of southern England suitable for breeding.

And what of the Black Kite? Well, large birds of prey are often reluctant to cross water, so the English Channel may present another barrier to this quirky but fascinating raptor. Or it may not. Earlier this spring, southern Britain experienced a minor invasion of kites, with as many as 30 wandering birds involved. Influxes like this are the result of 'overshooting', in which migrating birds returning from their African winter-quarters are encouraged to overfly their breeding grounds by the presence of an anticyclone to the south of Britain.

In one sense, overshooting birds are lost, but I prefer to think of them as pioneers, exploring the potential of new breeding areas beyond their normal range. If global warming makes these new areas suitable for colonisation, then we could yet see future wanderers settling down to breed in southern Britain. A century hence, birdwatchers in Sussex and Kent may be so used to the Black Kite that they hardly give it a second glance, as it rises into the clear skies of a warm July morning.

Birding with Donald Duck

 NOVEMBER 1997

A trip to Florida gave me an ideal chance to get to grips with a whole range of American birds – and I don't just mean Donald Duck. Although come to think of it, Disney World is as good a place to start as any.

The first decision: should you take the boat or monorail to the fabulous Magic Kingdom? The monorail may be quicker, but for sheer spectacle the boat wins out every time. Not only do the kids get their first view of Tinkerbell's castle, but dad can try out his bird identification skills.

That snow-white apparition on the edge of the lake? A Great Egret. The flock of birds swimming on the water? American Coots. And that strange creature perched on the landing-jetty? An Anhinga, whose long, graceful neck makes it look more like a reptile than a bird. Once inside Disney World, it's worth spending a bit of time watching the antics of the starling-like grackles, as they swoop down to snatch every crumb of spilt food. No wonder the place is so clean.

The Kennedy Space Center is another must. As we drove across the flat, swampy land approaching Cape Canaveral, flocks of Turkey Vultures were already rising in the sky, on the heat generated by the early-morning sun. And yes, just like the Wild West movies, vultures really do circle overhead, as if they're waiting for a cowboy to die.

As I parked the car, I had an even greater surprise – the silhouette of a Bald Eagle, lifting its heavy body into the sky on broad wings.

Bald Eagles once faced extinction in the eastern US, because of persecution and pesticides. But America's national bird has made an astonishing comeback, and today eagles can be seen throughout Florida.

Sanibel Island is worth a visit for all sorts of reasons: beautiful beaches, fine fish restaurants and, of course, birds. We took a bike ride around the famous Ding Darling Wildlife Refuge, home to alligators, ten different species of heron, and what my son James called 'strawberry yogurt birds' – the impossibly pink Roseate Spoonbills.

Not that you have to make such an effort. You could just sip margaritas by the hotel pool, watching Brown Pelicans flap by on their vast wings, while Ospreys plunge into the sea for fish. That's the great thing about Florida – it's all so easy. OK, so I made a bit of an effort – taking a couple of half-day birding trips with my friend Bill Pranty, author of the essential *Birder's Guide to Florida*. (And yes, for all you hard-core birders out there, we did see a Red-cockaded Woodpecker!) But to be honest, without really trying, even a newcomer to American birding can see well over a hundred species in a fortnight.

So what was my most treasured memory? A boardwalk in the wood by Sanibel's lighthouse, an hour or so before dusk. Once I was sure I was alone, I tried my hand at 'pishing', the bizarre method of birdcalling favoured by many American birders. At first, the trees stayed silent, as if mocking my amateur technique. Then, a single bird hopped out onto the forest floor beneath the boardwalk.

It was a female American Redstart, a late migrant on its way south for the winter. For 20 minutes or more it flew around below me, twirling from side to side, constantly flicking its tail to reveal gorgeous yellow patches. Most of the time it was too close for me to focus my binoculars. So I simply stood and watched, marvelling at the beauty of this tiny creature.

Its tameness was a humbling reminder that humans are relative newcomers here, and that not so very long ago this vast continent belonged exclusively to nature. What a contrast with a foggy dawn a couple of days later, as the weak November sun rose above the M25, and Wood Pigeons flocked in the frosty fields.

The Promised Land

 JANUARY 1998

If you ask any British birdwatcher where to go to see large numbers of migrating birds, one place they would certainly recommend is Israel's best-known holiday resort, Eilat. Situated by the Red Sea, Eilat lies on a major crossroads for birds heading south from their European and Asian breeding grounds to winter in Africa.

But not all birds go quite so far. Many millions spend the whole winter in Israel, in the verdant valleys of Galilee and the River Jordan. Northern Israel offers some of the most spectacular winter birding anywhere in the world, although to most British birders, it remains unfamiliar.

In the last week of November, I spent six hectic days travelling the length of Israel, on a recce for the new series of *Birding with Bill Oddie*. The birding was superb: both in terms of the variety of species and sheer numbers.

We began in the Hula Valley, deep in the heart of Galilee. It was one of those days when the birds just keep on coming, and it's hard to know where to look next. First, a flock of White Pelicans, fishing in unison like a team of synchronised swimmers. Then, the raptors: Black Kites, Marsh Harriers and Long-legged Buzzards, and the unmistakable shape of my first ever Greater Spotted Eagle, the first of five different eagle species recorded that day.

We also visited the gorge at Gamla in the Golan Heights. Raptors are usually seen high in the sky, so watching vast Griffon Vultures soaring beneath us in the gorge itself was a novel experience. With them were flocks of Little Swifts: miniature, stubby-looking versions of our familiar species.

Mount Hermon, in the extreme north, is quite unlike any other habitat in Israel, and as a result has birds found nowhere else in the country. Among the boulders, we searched for the aptly named Rock Nuthatch, eventually located by its piping call. In a nearby valley we also found two or three Sombre Tits, their black, white and brown plumage reminding me of a giant version of our Coal Tit.

Next day we were at Kefar Rupim in the Jordan Valley, whose fishponds support incredible numbers of waterbirds. Kingfishers were everywhere: not just our common version, but hovering Pied and splendid White-breasted Kingfishers, too.

Flocks of egrets and storks – Black and White – thronged the ponds themselves, attracted by the abundant food supplies. And deep in the reedbed we discovered a local speciality, Clamorous Reed Warbler – looking just like our own species, but about twice as big!

Travelling south, we soon reached the Dead Sea. We stopped to watch flocks of Tristram's Grackles, whose wolf-whistling calls echo round the gardens of the luxury hotels. We also saw Fan-tailed Ravens, possibly the very species sent out by Noah to search for dry land during the Flood.

Winter is not the best time to look for birds in Eilat, although we did see a splendid Imperial Eagle, a flock of Greater Flamingos on the saltpans, and groups of dazzling Little Green Bee-eaters.

But the experience which will stay longest in my memory came on our very first evening in Israel, as we stood by the side of a field in the Hula Valley. As dusk fell, the vast flocks of cranes feeding in the fields began to go to roost. Perhaps because of their huge size and upright stance, cranes have a special affinity with people. All over the world, they are threatened with loss of their vital wetland habitats, so it was comforting to see upwards of 20,000 birds in this one place. As they passed overhead, they filled the sky with their broad wings and deep, honking calls in an awesome spectacle.

Trinidad: the silent forest

 FEBRUARY 1998

Nothing stirred in the forest: no sound, no movement. Yet Kenny, our guide, had somehow sensed the presence of a bird among the leaf-litter on the forest floor. Quietly, he turned and gestured to a spot a few metres in front of us. I lifted my binoculars, adjusted the focus, and it was there. A tiny, wren-like bird, patiently picking through the carpet of leaves in search of food. Rufous back, black face and throat, and white underparts: a White-bellied Antbird. For a few moments, before it disappeared from view, we enjoyed the privilege of watching this secretive little creature going about its business. Then, it was gone, and we were back to reality.

I say reality, but the sense of being in another world rarely went away. I was leading a small group of British birdwatchers on a fortnight's trip to Trinidad & Tobago. T&T, as the regulars say, are two islands just off the north-east coast of South America. Their proximity to this vast continent means that the birdlife is very different from the rest of the Caribbean and has more in common with nearby Venezuela.

For the newcomer to this region, T&T provide the perfect introduction to neotropical birding, without the difficulties found on the South American mainland. You can see species from most major South American bird families, without the bewildering variety you get in Peru or Brazil. The locals even speak English, play cricket and drive on the left!

On Trinidad we stayed at the Pax Guest House, under the care and attention of the delightful Gerard and Oda Ramsawak. Sipping a Carib beer on the terrace at Pax, while ten different kinds of raptor soar overhead, is about as easy and pleasurable as birding can get. At Pax we also got to know the species we were to see every day: the beautiful Blue-gray Tanager, the noisy Great Kiskadee and the delightful

Copper-rumped Hummingbird, which perched on a twig just by the terrace to give excellent close-up views.

Later on the first morning we ventured into the jungle. Jungle birding is quite unlike any other kind. You walk in single file along a path, watching and listening intently. At first, it seems as if nothing is stirring, but suddenly you see a brief movement in the thick foliage. Nine times out of ten you fail to make contact with the bird itself, so when you finally do, you certainly feel you've earned it.

We also spent a day in the wetlands, first at the Pointe-à-Pierre Wildfowl Trust, where we got fabulous views of a Green Kingfisher and the dazzling yellow Saffron Finch; then by the sea at Waterloo, where vast flocks of gulls, terns and waders were joined by Black Skimmers, living up to their name by dipping their beaks into the water to pick up morsels of food.

But it was to the jungle that we kept returning, under Kenny's expert guidance. The final day on Trinidad was the most memorable, as by now we knew which species would be hardest to find. Patiently, Kenny located one target bird after another: first a multicoloured Trinidad Euphonia, then the secretive Great Antshrike. But at this high altitude the real prizes are the trogons, the quintessential birds of the tropical rainforest.

Time after time, Kenny mimicked the haunting call of the Collared Trogon. Time and again, the bird responded, although we could see no movement in the forest canopy. I was tempted to call it a day. But Kenny wasn't going to be beaten, and at long last his faith was justified.

As if from nowhere, a stunningly beautiful bird appeared perched on a horizontal branch. Bright green head, breast and back contrasted with vivid scarlet underparts. But it was the tail that caught the attention: impossibly long and delicately barred black and white. We stood and watched, hardly daring to speak, as the bird called a few times. It flew from branch to branch, before melting back into the rainforest. Followed by stillness. And silence.

Teatime on Tobago

 MARCH 1998

Visiting the island of Tobago is rather like going back 30 years or so. The people are well-dressed and courteous, the beaches are unspoilt and the sea is so clear you could have a bath in it. And every day, at 4.30 p.m. on the dot, you can take afternoon tea on the terrace of the Arnos Vale Hotel.

If you do, you won't be alone. Almost as soon as the neat plate of sandwiches and cake arrives at your table, you're sure to be joined by an uninvited guest with an unforgettable name: the Bananaquit. This little bird is the House Sparrow of the neotropics. Ubiquitous, cheeky and always on the lookout for a meal, he and his companions may also join you for breakfast, where they flit from table to table picking out the choicest items from the buffet.

Bananaquits aren't the only birds to benefit from the open-handed generosity of the Arnos Vale and its guests. The hotel staff regularly fill a large plastic trough with leftovers, attracting a colourful cross-section of the island's commoner species.

First to arrive will be two or three Eared Doves, looking like a miniature version of our Collared Dove, but with the small dark mark behind the eye which gives the species its name. They'll soon be joined by vivid Blue-gray Tanagers, one of the loveliest of all neotropical birds, along with their drabber cousins, Palm Tanagers. Occasionally a Red-crowned Woodpecker will attempt to hang on to the edge of the trough, desperately trying to raise itself up like an out-of-condition gymnast, before slipping away unsatisfied to feed elsewhere.

A plaintive mewing sound, uncannily like that of a domestic cat, marks the arrival of the rather pathetic-looking Bare-eyed Thrush. And from time to time, a cracking little black-and-white striped creature known to the locals as the 'jailbird' will appear. It's officially called the Barred Antshrike, but the local name is a far more evocative description of its pied appearance.

But all these birds, attractive as they are, are overshadowed by two show-stoppers. The first, the Blue-crowned Motmot, is simply one of the most colourful birds I have ever seen: a gorgeous mixture of green, chestnut, blue and black, with a hefty beak and long, twin-plumed tail. The local motmots are said to have developed a liking for cocktail cherries, something we failed to test out, owing to an inexplicable shortage of supplies.

The other Tobago speciality looks, at first sight, like a cross between a turkey and a pheasant. Only a minute or two after the food has been put out, Rufous-vented Chachalacas arrive en masse at the feeding-station. As they do so, they squabble noisily among themselves, pushing and shoving each other aside in order to get to their supper.

It's only when things start to get nasty, and the pushing and shoving turns into out-and-out violence, that you recall what these peculiar birds really remind you of. Everything about their appearance and behaviour is uncannily reminiscent of those nasty little dinosaurs in the film *Jurassic Park*. The ones that hop up and down in a curiously engaging manner, before tearing your flesh into tiny pieces.

Big Bird Diary

SEPTEMBER 1998

As I write, I can hear the deep, bass notes of a Ground Hornbill in the distant forest. Breakfast this morning was interrupted by a passing African Fish Eagle. And yesterday I came across one of the most extraordinary birds I've ever seen – the multicoloured Hartlaub's Turaco.

By now, you may have guessed that I've ventured a little further afield than usual. I'm in the Masai Mara, Kenya, filming the new series of *Big Cat Diary*. Kenya is one of the very best countries in the world to watch birds. More than a thousand species have been recorded here, and it is possible to see over three hundred in a single day! Yet after almost two weeks, I've barely topped the century mark.

The reason for this rather poor showing is that I've been mainly confined to our base at Governors' Paradise Camp, alongside the Mara River. Fortunately, if I were to choose a place to get stuck, this would be it. I am lulled to sleep at night by the snorting of hippos, while this morning a herd of elephants wandered down to the river to drink. Crocodiles and baboons regularly appear on the far bank to entertain us.

And, of course, there are the birds. Woodland Kingfishers often fly up and down the river, while overhead there are three species of vulture, five different kinds of swallow and passing flocks of Yellow-billed and Marabou Storks.

On my first morning here, I awoke to what I thought was a familiar sound: the 'jug-jug-jug' of a Nightingale. Within seconds, it abruptly changed to impersonate a Blackbird, then a Song Thrush. I wandered out of the tent, and there, on a low branch, was a thrush-sized bird with rusty-orange underparts, slate-grey back and a striking black-and-white head-pattern. It was a White-browed Robin-chat, just one of the many songbirds whose dawn chorus starts our day.

Some of the birds here are old friends, such as the little Common Sandpiper which feeds along the water's edge, keeping a wary eye out for passing crocodiles. A black-and-white bird with a long, wagging tail looks familiar. But it's not our own species, rather its larger cousin, the African Pied Wagtail. Different bird, same habits.

Others are totally unfamiliar. Pairs of Tropical Boubous sing the most extraordinary four-note duet: the male taking the first two notes, while his partner responds immediately with notes three and four. Two species of hornbills: the huge Ground Hornbill and its smaller, tree-dwelling relative. And that extraordinary turaco.

I was on a lunchtime walk. Well, I say walk, but what I really mean is a short stroll along the front of the tents – to go any further into the forest would risk attack from a stray buffalo or elephant. As I reached the end of the path, a bird flew across the river. I raised my binoculars, and my eyes were assaulted by a flash of red: so deep, so crimson, that I thought I must be dreaming. It landed in a tree, and I saw a moss-green bird the size of a small pheasant, with a long tail, short crest and comic expression. It turned and then flew again, to reveal the crimson wing-linings once more. Hartlaub's Turaco: what a bird!

Birding at leisure

 OCTOBER 1998

There can't be many places in the world where you can sip fresh Kenyan coffee, enjoy a *pain au chocolat* and watch some of the rarest and most exotic birds imaginable. So after seven weeks without a break, it was good to escape from the BBC's Big Cat Diary camp and have a leisurely breakfast at Little Governors' Safari Camp, in the heart of the Masai Mara.

The table overlooks a marsh, where Holub's Golden Weavers cling to the tops of reeds, Black Crakes clamber across waterlogged vegetation, and dashing Purple Grenadiers hop around on the lawn. After breakfast, we took a stroll with Mark, the camp's resident balloonist and an ace birder. We wandered through a troop of baboons and past the rubbish dump to reach an oxbow lake, formed last winter when the Mara River burst its banks.

There, in a tree, was a pair of huge birds, with pied plumage and the most extraordinary bill I've ever seen. They were Black-and-white Casqued Hornbills: sporting the horny protuberance on top of their beaks that gives the species its name. Around the lake there were Hooded Vultures, rising on the first thermals of the day; the resident Woodland Kingfisher, a splash of blue among the browns and greens;

and the usual Yellow-vented Bulbuls, which have the annoying ability to look like something new and exciting, before revealing their true identity.

We then took a ride across the Mara to Kichwa Tembo Camp. This may be as close as you can get to paradise, with fine food, a swimming pool and a couple of dozen new species to see during the day. We walked around the grounds with the camp's naturalist guide, Philip, a man with the necessary combination of local knowledge, fieldcraft and quiet enthusiasm to make it an afternoon to remember.

At first, the forest seemed almost birdless, making me feel quite at home. Then we came across a fruiting tree, alive with birds. African Paradise Flycatchers, with deep rufous-and-black plumage and an impossibly long tail; a Grey Apalis, looking for all the world like a Lesser Whitethroat; and best of all, a Black Cuckoo-shrike, with its smart blue-black plumage and bright yellow epaulettes.

Deeper in the forest, we heard the call of Schalow's Turaco and caught a frustratingly brief glimpse of the bird itself in flight. We had better luck with a pair of Ross's Turacos, whose deep-blue plumage, raised crest and bright yellow face give them the comical appearance of a children's TV character.

But best of all was a Narina Trogon. The name 'trogon' has always suggested to me something in *Dr Who* – 'welcome to the planet Trogon, doctor . . .' I've watched three different species in Trinidad, and was surprised to find that the family is not confined to South America but can be found throughout the tropics. Narina Trogon is one of two trogons found in Kenya, and was apparently named after the wife of the man who first discovered the species.

Philip began by imitating the trogon's call: a surprisingly muted series of low, bass notes, almost inaudible to the human ear. From the depths of the forest, the bird responded. It sounded as if it were about half a mile away, but to our surprise, Philip pointed out a movement in the nearby trees. There, perched on a branch, was a vision of scarlet and green, with a bright yellow beak, pale eye-patch and long black-and-white tail. As we watched, it started to call: quietly at first, then gradually turning up the volume as it began to speed up. Narina must have been proud to have such a beautiful bird named after her.

A walk on the wild side

 NOVEMBER 1998

If you wanted to go for a quiet country stroll, the Masai Mara isn't the first place you'd consider. For a start, it is home to one of the largest concentrations of predators in the world, with the 'big three' – Lion, Leopard and Cheetah – at the top of the food chain. The Mara also supports herds of elephants, wandering bands of hyenas and large numbers of buffaloes – often considered to be Africa's most dangerous wild animal.

So when Colin, the safari guide at Governors' Camp, asked me if I wanted to go on a walk, I thought he was joking. I called his bluff, and the next day found myself in the back seat of a Land Rover, bumping along the waterlogged, pot-holed track which leads away from the camp and into the Mara Game Reserve.

Walking – or even getting out of your vehicle at all – is strictly forbidden in the reserve itself, so we drove for about 45 minutes until we were beyond its boundaries. Then Colin stopped the vehicle, and we got out and started to walk.

On foot, you see the Mara from a completely different perspective. For a start, you get an unencumbered view of the skies, enabling me to spot majestic Bateleur Eagles as they soared high overhead. With the engine turned off, I could also hear birdsong, with the fluty notes of glossy starlings mingling with the scratchy sound of cisticolas – Africa's archetypal 'little brown jobs'.

From a birder's point of view, Kenya offers a delightful mix of the exotic and the everyday. Lilac-breasted Rollers, with their dazzling blue and purple plumage, perch on the tops of acacias, while migrant European Wheatears hop around on the ground beneath. I saw a quick movement in a bush and discovered a Willow Warbler, perhaps the bird I'd been watching on my local patch in London a couple of months before. Meanwhile, flocks of swallows hawked for insects low over our heads.

Not every bird is quite so familiar. A pair of tiny finches landed in front of me, revealing a dazzling blue plumage, with bright red patches beneath their eyes. Like many African species, this little bird sports an improbably exotic name: Red-cheeked Cordon-bleu.

One of my companions, who had at first claimed to have no interest in birds, was rapidly becoming hooked. He drew my attention to an even more brightly coloured bird, hopping around on the short grass. It was clearly a bunting, with a black-and-white striped head and deep golden-yellow underparts – but which species? To find out its identity, I rapidly extricated the massive *Birds of Kenya and Northern Tanzania* from my rucksack, turned to plate 121 and identified the bird as a Golden-breasted Bunting. This wonderful book is the key reference work for visiting birders, though it weighs several kilos, so you need to be both fit and dedicated to take it into the field.

Whenever there were few birds to see, Colin kept us entertained by pointing out the plant and insect life, even getting us to sample some, including a hot, peppermint-flavoured leaf used by the Masai as toothpaste. He also spotted a dark bird of prey with a comical hairstyle: the aptly named Long-crested Eagle. As we approached, we realised the bird was in the process of eating a large rat. First, it swallowed the prey whole, then regurgitated the unfortunate rodent; finally it swallowed it whole once again, before flying off. By the time we reached our vehicle, where Colin opened a couple of bottles of Tusker lager, the sun was already setting.

Miracle in the Holy Land

 FEBRUARY 1999

'These birds are like politicians,' said David Glasner, director of the Jordan Valley Birdwatching Centre in northern Israel. 'They make a lot of noise, but soon as you try to get near them, they disappear.' The bird in question was the Black Francolin, a handsome but elusive member of the partridge family (the bird, not the pop group). I was on my fifth birding trip to Israel, filming the latest *Birding with Bill Oddie*, and the Black Francolin was fast becoming my 'bogey bird'.

The following morning, we made an early start, heading towards the kibbutz at Kefar Rupim for an appetising breakfast of hard-boiled eggs, pickled herring and cucumbers. As usual, the film crew were in the vehicle in front, speeding along ahead of me.

Suddenly their minibus screeched to a halt. I grabbed the walkie-talkie and called them, expecting the worst. But before I could make contact, a bird closely resembling a domestic chicken walked out from behind the minibus's front wheel. Yes, it was a Black Francolin. My duck – if you'll pardon the expression – had been broken at last.

The francolin's brush with death raised an interesting question. If the crew had actually run it over, would I have been able to count the bird on my life list? Probably not, but in the context of a trip like this it hardly mattered: there were more than enough birds to keep us all happy.

Bill had only been to Israel twice before, so he was picking up several new species, including a stunning male Sinai Rosefinch in the hills above Eilat. And on a trip to the Negev Desert, in the company of top Israeli birder Hadoram Shirihai, we came across a huge female Saker Falcon perched on top of an electricity pylon.

But for me, the best thing about having been here so many times before is that I don't need to worry about seeing new birds – I can just sit back and enjoy the old ones. Every visit is different, and this time I had the chance to explore the green valleys of the north, with their astonishing wealth of wintering birds.

At the fishponds in the Jordan Valley, waterbirds are the main attraction, with flocks of White and Black Storks, hordes of egrets and Spoonbills, and a fascinating selection of gulls, including Caspian, Armenian and the magnificent Great Black-headed.

It's true that most British birders still visit southern Israel in spring and autumn, to witness the twice-annual migration. But for me, a winter visit to the far north – the Hula Valley in Galilee – is just as enjoyable. The profusion of birds here is truly biblical: vast numbers of pelicans and cranes compete for your attention with more than a dozen different birds of prey, including the rare Pallid Harrier and Greater Spotted Eagle.

The day we arrived, the first rains of the winter began, shrouding the valley in a pall of grey. At first we were disappointed, fearing we might not be able to get the footage we needed to complete the programme. But in true British tradition we pressed on regardless, and, fortunately, luck was on our side. On the first afternoon, the rain stopped an hour or so before dusk, and we watched squadrons of White Pelicans cruising low over the reeds on their way to roost.

The next day was our last in Israel, and again we suffered from a mid-afternoon downpour. Then, just as we were about to give up, the skies cleared, and the rain stopped. A rainbow appeared against the dark grey sky, and a beam of sunshine came down from the heavens. As if on cue, a huge flock of cranes took off against this stunning backdrop, uttering their haunting calls as they flew. It may not have been a miracle, but for me, it certainly felt like one.

Going Dutch

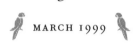 MARCH 1999

If you want to see a million geese of a dozen different species, with a whole host of other wintering birds, then Holland is definitely the place to go. If, like me, you live in south-east England, then it's actually easier to reach than most British goose haunts. You just pop through the Channel Tunnel, turn left, and three hours later you're watching the birds.

Wherever you go, the old rubs shoulders with the new, as ancient windmills stand alongside sleek modern wind turbines. The whole place has a strange beauty – though perhaps rather more strange than beautiful. After a while you long to get a view from high ground, or a few hills to break the visual monotony.

But Holland's birdlife is far from monotonous. Any time of year is good for a visit, but winter is truly special. Huge flocks of geese feed in the fields, chomping away at the crops while trampling them with their feet – much to the annoyance of local farmers. On the IJsselmeer, a man-made lake so large it's like a small sea, there are vast flocks of duck – often so distant you can barely identify the species.

Once again, I was with a camera crew filming the latest series of *Birding with Bill Oddie*. We began our trip in the south, in the region of Zeeland, which literally means 'sea land'. Much of this area is reclaimed and is rich in nutrients for crops and geese alike. The two commonest goose species were Barnacle and White-fronted, though we also saw Bean, Greylag, Brent and Pink-footed, together with odd-ities such as vagrant Lesser White-fronts, dubious-looking Canada Geese and even more peculiar hybrids.

Next to the world's biggest harbour, Europoort, a wintering flock of tiny birds took to the air, giving their characteristic tinkling call. They were Snow Buntings, looking like little angels, especially when they flew against the rapidly setting sun. With them was a small group of Shore Larks, showing their splendid black and yellow face pattern and the tiny 'horns' that give them their alternative name, Horned Lark.

On Sunday morning, a pre-dawn start took us to a wooded park on the outskirts of Haarlem, one of the most densely populated areas of Europe. A fall of snow the previous week had yet to melt, giving the place a wonderfully wintry atmosphere. Fortunately we had beaten the joggers and dog-walkers, and were rewarded by the comical sight of a Black Woodpecker poking its head out of the roost-hole. It eyed us suspiciously, before flying off, uttering a curious high-pitched call as it went.

Despite this part of Holland being so close to East Anglia, Black Woodpecker has yet to be officially recorded in Britain. In recent years, however, it has been spreading northwards and westwards, so it's well worth looking out for this magnificent creature, the largest of Europe's woodpeckers.

Another species hardly ever found in Britain was everywhere. Short-toed Treecreeper is barely distinguishable in the field from its common relative: except, that is, for the distinctive call, which we could hear loud and clear on this bright winter's morning.

That afternoon we headed north, into Friesland. As we drove along the long, exposed dyke across the IJsselmeer, the weather rapidly took a turn for the worse. We found ourselves shivering in the wind-chill as we watched Barnacle Geese feeding in the snowy fields. While we were filming yet another flock of geese, Richard, the camera assistant, drew my attention to a bulky brown bird flying past. It was a Bittern, a rare sight anywhere, and always a delight to see. Rarely can a wild goose chase have been so productive and enjoyable.

Spring in the Med

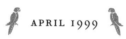 APRIL 1999

Mallorca might not be the first place you'd think of when planning a birding holiday abroad – but it certainly should be. Cheap flights, a thriving tourist industry and a variety of habitats make it an ideal destination for a first trip outside the UK.

Although Mallorca is good for birds at any time of year, the peak season is definitely spring, when huge numbers of migrants cross the Mediterranean on their way north to breed. I'll be going back there with a film crew later this month, but I had a sneak preview just before Easter, when I visited the island with my 11-year-old son David who isn't a great fan of birdwatching. I knew it could be an uphill struggle, but he tagged along with a modicum of good grace, indulging me in what he considers to be a bizarre and eccentric pastime.

I bumped into one of my target species on our very first evening, as we wandered along the sea-front at Port de Pollença. A closer look at the birds on the beach revealed them to be Audouin's Gulls, one of the rarest of their family. Their blood-red bill and rather haughty stance marked them off from their commoner counterparts. Audouin's Gull has done rather well recently, but even so I didn't expect to see them pottering about in the middle of this busy resort.

The next day we visited two of Mallorca's best-known sites. We spent the morning in the Boquer Valley, where we watched a Hoopoe bringing back food to its young – proving that the breeding season here kicks off a lot earlier than back home. That evening, we strolled around the Albufereta Marsh, though unfortunately we were a week or so early for most migrants. In compensation the two resident warblers, Fan-tailed and Cetti's, competed with each other in volume, with Cetti's winning by a few decibels.

Every birding hotspot has its local expert, and Mallorca is no exception. Graham Hearl has been visiting the island for almost three decades, and a few years ago he took the plunge and came to live here permanently. Graham's greatest service to visiting birders is his excellent *Birdwatching Guide to Mallorca*, which gives step-by-step directions to the best sites on the island.

On a fine, sunny morning, he took us up a scenic, winding road, leading into the mountains. At first, we scanned the deep blue skies without much success, but as we sat down to eat our packed lunch we had excellent views of Black Vultures, one of Europe's largest flying birds. This magnificent raptor once almost went extinct in Mallorca, but thanks to a reintroduction project there is now a healthy breeding population on the island.

We also spent a day at S'Albufera, Mallorca's premier reserve. Despite lying just outside the tourist hotspot of Alcudia, the Albufera is one of the very best wetlands in the whole of the Mediterranean. Moustached Warblers skulk deep in the reedbeds, while Kentish Plovers and Black-winged Stilts feed on every patch of mud.

My 'target bird' here was another reintroduction, the bizarre Purple Swamphen. This giant relative of the Coot and Moorhen was a particular favourite with the Romans, who prized its tender flesh, but it died out here during the nineteenth century. Now it thrives, unharmed, in the safety of the reserve.

On our final day we headed south, to the windswept Cabo de Salinas, where we watched distant Cory's and Balearic Shearwaters gliding across the waves. Later, at nearby Cabo Blanco, I finally caught up with two elusive Mallorcan specialities. Thekla Larks were fairly easy to see as they sung from bushes and telegraph wires. Marmora's Warbler proved much harder to pin down, but we finally heard its distinctive scratchy song and caught a glimpse of this western Mediterranean endemic, a darker version of our own Dartford Warbler.

As a starter, this was great, but I can't wait to get back in a week or so to witness the wonders of spring migration. By the way, David enjoyed his trip – even if he still can't understand why his dad is so fascinated by birds.

The naming of birds

 MAY 1999

Eleonora of Arborea was, by all accounts, a remarkable woman. Fourteenth-century Sardinia wasn't exactly a bastion of sexual equality, yet Eleonora triumphed against the odds to become ruler of the island. Even today, almost 600 years after her death, she is hailed as Sardinia's national heroine.

It's a nice story, but what does it have to do with birding in Mallorca? Only that one of the most sought-after birds on the island is a long-winged, slim and elegant bird of prey, named after the Sardinian monarch herself. And like its eponymous heroine, Eleonora's Falcon is a remarkable bird. It spends the winter months in Madagascar, and returns to islands around the Mediterranean during the last week of April or first week of May.

But unlike most migrants, it doesn't begin courtship and nesting the moment it gets back. Instead, it waits until July or even August before breeding. By this unusual evolutionary strategy the adults are able to feed their growing chicks on songbird migrants as they return south during September and October.

It wasn't until the very last day of filming in Mallorca that the *Birding with Bill Oddie* team finally managed to find Eleonora's Falcon. We were walking along the Boquer Valley, in the north of the island, when we noticed what looked like a flock of Swifts high over the hills above. A closer look revealed the unmistakable shape of hunting falcons: the Eleonora's were back!

Eleonora's Falcon isn't the only Mallorcan speciality named after a historical figure. Indeed, of the four other 'target birds' which every visitor to the island wants to see, only one, Black Vulture, is not. After a fair amount of effort, we not only saw the other three, but captured them on video too.

The first, Audouin's Gull, was fairly easy to film, as one bird had the habit of wandering up and down the beach opposite the Hotel Pollentia each morning. One of the world's rarest gulls, it has a peculiar, rather fastidious walk, looking down its beak at you as if questioning your right to share the same stretch of sand.

Audouin's Gull shows up the tit-for-tat nature of the way birds are often named. It was discovered in Sardinia by a French ornithologist, Monsieur Payraudeau, who named it after his colleague in Paris, Jean Victor Audouin. Perhaps Payraudeau was hoping Audouin would return the compliment, but unfortunately he failed to take the hint, and while Audouin's name is forever linked to this elegant gull, Payraudeau's is long forgotten.

In a nice historical connection, Marmora's Warbler was named after the nineteenth-century Italian ornithologist who discovered Eleonora's Falcon, Alberto della Marmora. The bird itself is a skulking little warbler which dwells in 'garrigue', the mile after mile of thorny scrub which hugs the coast like a blanket. Like Eleonora's Falcon and Audouin's Gull, Marmora's Warbler has a very restricted range, being confined to a few scattered locations in the western Mediterranean.

The final member of the quartet lives in the garrigue too. Thekla Lark is a fairly nondescript, small, brown bird, looking like a plump, crested Skylark. However, its name conceals the most touching story of all. Thekla Brehm was the only girl in a family of seven children born to the eminent German ornithologist Christian Ludwig Brehm. Unfortunately, she died in her early twenties from heart disease, in 1857. In the meantime, her two older brothers had been on an expedition to Spain, during which they had 'collected' a previously unknown species of lark. Her grief-stricken father named the bird after his beloved daughter, granting Thekla a little piece of immortality.

An Aquatic lifestyle

 JUNE 1999

My son's *Pocket Oxford Dictionary* defines the word 'aquatic' as 'living in or on water'. So it may come as a surprise that there is a species of bird named Aquatic Warbler. If this conjures up an image of a little brown bird living in a swamp and wearing a snorkel and flippers, this isn't too far from the truth.

Aquatic Warbler has the unenviable distinction of being Europe's rarest migratory songbird. As a breeding species, it is confined to a narrow zone stretching from the former East Germany to the River Ob in western Siberia. At the heart of this range lies its stronghold: the wetlands of eastern Poland.

It was here in the Biebrza Marshes, on a wet and windy morning, that I finally managed to get good views of this elusive little bird. We were driving along in an old Chevy van with top Polish bird guide Marek Borkowski, when he stopped by the side of what looked like an overgrown, weedy field.

Our first reaction was surprise: why would one of Europe's rarest birds choose to live in this undistinguished looking habitat? Once we ventured closer, though, we could see why Marek had insisted we wore Wellington boots. The 'field' was in fact submerged under almost a foot of water, out of which protruded rank grass and sedges, along with a few scattered, stunted bushes.

It didn't look as if any bird could survive in such a bizarre, watery environment. But then, above the sound of Skylarks and Meadow Pipits, we heard a short but distinctive song, described by my companion Derek as sounding like a cross between a rattle and a canary. We stopped to listen, hampered by the rain and wind. I gazed over the distant sedges, straining to see a buff-coloured bird against buff-coloured vegetation. Suddenly, I caught a movement out of the corner of my eye. Just a few metres in front of us, on a stem barely protruding above the water, was our prize: a singing male Aquatic Warbler.

One challenge had already been achieved: to see the bird. Now we faced an even greater one: to capture it on video. Immediately we went into action: I jammed the heavy tripod into the swampy ground, Derek used his ample frame and an umbrella to shield the camera from the wind, while cameraman Andrew adjusted focus and exposure and pressed the 'on' button. The tape began to run.

We held our breath, not daring to ask if the image passed Andrew's seriously high standards. A minute or so later the bird ducked down out of view, and he gave his verdict: 'Stonking. Eight out of ten'. High praise indeed: and quite possibly the first time Aquatic Warbler has been captured on video.

Once the breeding season is over, Aquatic Warblers take a rather unorthodox migration route westwards, through the Low Countries and France, to their winter-quarters somewhere in western Africa. Each year, a few birds cross the Channel, turning up at south coast sites such as Radipole Lake and Marazion Marsh. It was here, almost ten years ago, that I caught a brief glimpse of three tawny-yellow juveniles, my first encounter with the species.

Of all the regular visitors to our shores, Aquatic Warbler is surely one of the least known. Its skulking habits don't advertise its presence, and it lacks the appeal of other, more glamorous, endangered species. But the very existence of this little bird at the end of the twentieth century represents a triumph of biodiversity over human interference. It has evolved to live in one of Europe's most unusual habitats, and despite a long-term decline, continues to hang on by a thread in its marshy home. For this feat alone, Aquatic Warbler deserves to survive.

Beside the seaside – Stateside

 SEPTEMBER 1999

Last month I took my son James on a trip to a Victorian seaside resort.
We swam in the sea, played crazy golf and had breakfast at a beach-
front café. During the trip I also managed to get a dozen lifers,
including two waders, a woodpecker, a tit, a swallow, a warbler, a sparrow and a finch. But despite the familiar ring to these birds, we weren't
visiting Brighton or Blackpool – or anywhere on this side of the
Atlantic – but Cape May, New Jersey, USA.

I love birding on the other side of the Atlantic. American birds are
a mirror image of European ones, with instantly recognisable families,
but a very different selection of species. As well as the everyday gulls,
terns and waders, we also saw waxwings, ibises, and even hummingbirds. The US gives you the best of both worlds: the birds aren't as
confusing as in the tropics, but they can be just as rewarding.

Take those hummingbirds. There was something surreal about
watching a Ruby-throated Hummingbird feeding from a nectar dis-
penser barely a couple of metres away, while I was sitting on a porch
drinking cranberry juice, in what looked like an English country
garden.

Pat and Clay Sutton's garden is justly famous as a haven for breeding
and migrating birds. So while James curled up in a comfy hammock,
I enjoyed views of a nesting Carolina Wren. Meanwhile, a Carolina
Chickadee called from the trees above, sounding uncannily like a Great
Tit. A sudden shower in this drought-parched landscape brought a
flurry of activity, with Yellow Warblers, American Redstarts and a
Cedar Waxwing – nothing out of the ordinary for the locals, but excit-
ing birds for me.

Meanwhile, the holidaymakers thronged the beaches, oblivious to
the presence of hundreds of Laughing Gulls, still sporting their dark-
hooded breeding plumage. A hundred years ago this was a rare bird on

the New Jersey coast, but thanks to its ability to live alongside people it is now one of the commonest.

Further along the shore, a thousand Sanderlings raced along the tideline, frantically feeding at this pit stop on their long journey from the Arctic to South America. James dug a trench in the wet sand, while I watched a single Piping Plover, a rare and vulnerable species which still nests in small numbers along this coast.

I finally managed to drag James away from the beach, and we walked through one of Cape May's best-known birding sites, the meadows. As virtually the only remaining wetland in the current drought, the meadows act as a magnet to migrant waders, or 'shore-birds', as they are known on this side of the pond.

The next day I took a guided walk around the meadows with Pete Dunne, director of Cape May Bird Observatory. Tall, good-looking and with a quiet air of authority, Pete is arguably the man most respon-sible for encouraging the growing popularity of birding in the US. He is also author of some of the best books ever written on the subject of why we watch birds.

This was the perfect opportunity to get to grips with difficult species such as Greater and Lesser Yellowlegs, Least and Semi-palmated Sandpipers, and the ultimate identification headache, Long-billed and Short-billed Dowitchers (no, the length of the bills isn't the best way to tell them apart . . .).

Later that day we called in at the bird observatory. James added a Bald Eagle to his collection of fluffy toys, while I got the latest birding info from observatory staffers Sheila and Marleen, as they answered an endless stream of telephone enquiries about birding. They told me what I already suspected: that although the birds were good in August, they would be even better in September, when I'll be back in Cape May. As they regaled me with tales of warbler, wader and raptor migration, I couldn't wait to return.

Very flat, Holland

 OCTOBER 1999

In the north of Holland, the sky and land and water melt into each other, and on a clear day the view seems to go on forever. There were lots of clear days in late August, when I visited the very first 'Top of Holland Bird Festival'. It was held in a field on the edge of the Lauwesmeer, a huge expanse of lakes and marshes by the North Sea. This is a great area for birds all year round, with vast flocks of geese in winter, singing Bluethroats in spring and hordes of migrants passing south in autumn.

From the festival site itself, we watched flocks of Spoonbills passing overhead, and Buzzards above the nearby wood. On a walk nearby we saw Caspian Terns, Spotted Crakes, and more than a dozen species of wader. Because the Netherlands are that little bit further east, Dutch birdlife is markedly different from back home: the commonest waders were Little Stints and Wood Sandpipers, and there wasn't a Dunlin to be seen.

A couple of miles up the road there stood a modern corporate building, all glass and steel, surrounded by a lake. There was a small crowd of cars, so we stopped and enquired if there was anything about. There certainly was: two minuscule Red-necked Phalaropes, stopping off on the long journey from the Arctic to their wintering grounds in the Arabian Sea. True to form, these peculiar little birds swam around in tight circles, frantically picking insects off the water surface with their needle-sharp bills.

Like its big brother, the British Birdwatching Fair, the festival itself boasted a mixture of the local and the global. Dutch birders mingled with visitors from five continents, as far away as Trinidad & Tobago, Jordan, Syria, Costa Rica and New Zealand.

After leaving the festival we headed south, stopping off to watch birds along the way. Despite being one of the most heavily populated regions on Earth, the central Netherlands is an excellent birding area. Flooded bulb fields were a magnet for more migrating waders, including large flocks of Curlew Sandpipers that look a bit like long-billed, oversized Dunlin. They undertake one of the most extraordinary journeys of all migrants: from their breeding grounds on the Siberian tundra, south and west through Europe, to spend the winter in Africa. Some autumns thousands pass through Britain; other years hardly any at all. Judging by the numbers we encountered, this has been a good breeding season.

As a final Continental fling before returning home, we stopped off at Le Portel, a seaside resort just outside Boulogne. This is one of the best places in Europe to get close-up views of Mediterranean Gulls – providing you've brought something to get their attention. Having forgotten to bring a loaf of bread, I improvised with a bar of chocolate. Gulls are nothing if not adaptable, and they soon developed a sweet tooth, flying up to grab the offering while giving feather-by-feather views.

Mediterranean Gull was once quite a rare bird in Europe, mainly confined to southern and eastern parts of the continent. Since the 1930s, however, it has spread north and west at a rapid rate, and has even begun to breed in the British Isles. So next time you see a flock of gulls, look for one with a blood-red bill, dark black hood and white wing-tips – and try offering it a piece of chocolate.

The wonder of warblers

NOVEMBER 1999

European warblers are a bit of an acquired taste. Their small size, muted colours and evasive habits make them difficult to identify even if you get a good view – and usually you don't. But though New World warblers share the elusive nature of their Old World cousins, they more than make up for this with their stunning colours.

Until I visited Cape May this autumn, I'd only seen a dozen of the 30 or so warbler species regularly found on the east coast of the US. In one memorable morning's birding I almost doubled this tally.

Not that it was easy. We started off on Higbees Dyke, arguably the best place to witness autumn songbird migration in the whole of North America. A cold front had passed the day before, followed by light north-westerly winds: ideal for what local expert Richard Crossley described as a flight. He had warned us to get up early and be on the dyke as the sun rose, at about half past six.

So there we were: a score of souls waiting in breathless anticipation of a birding spectacle to remember. With realism typical of his native Yorkshire, Richard warned us that things might not go according to plan. Like migrating songbirds everywhere, warblers are anything but predictable, and we feared that the whole event might be a sad anticlimax.

Then a dot flew over our heads. Followed by another. And another. The flight had begun. My first reaction was panic: how could I hope to identify these airborne specks, especially as there were several species I had never seen before? The locals held no such fears, and a steady chorus of name-checks hit the autumnal air. Wilson's, Yellow, Prairie, Black-throated Blue, Blackpoll... the list went on and on. Occasionally other birds were seen: orioles, tanagers and chunky Rose-breasted Grosbeaks – even a tiny Red-breasted Nuthatch that almost landed on our heads as it passed.

By now, two things were working to my advantage: the light was better, and I was starting to feel more confidence in my identification skills. As the warblers flew only yards above us, I could make out the black undertail of Magnolia, the humbug-like appearance of Black-and-white, and the distinctive jizz of Northern Waterthrush. Occasionally there would be one which baffled me completely, until I was rescued by Richard's confident call of a scarcer species such as Worm-eating Warbler.

After an hour that combined elation and bewilderment in roughly equal quantities, the flight stopped, almost as abruptly as it had begun.

Now was the time to comb the fields and woods, to try to get a better look at the birds we had seen passing overhead.

Providing you get decent views, New World warblers are not that difficult to identify – but some species are so elusive they can easily be overlooked. Fortunately I had excellent guides. As well as Richard, whose ability to find these birds verges on the supernatural, there was Sean, a newly arrived visitor from Ireland, who was as keen to reacquaint himself with past favourites as I was to see them for the first time.

We spent two hours looking, listening, pishing and squeaking – using everything in the birder's armoury to pin down these shy little creatures. By the end we had come across a total of 20 different species of warbler – a far cry from Cape May's record of over 30 in a day, but more than enough to keep me happy. A visit to the Ocean View provided a welcome end to the excursion: two eggs over easy, crispy bacon and a steaming plate of pancakes.

Jolly English weather

 JUNE 2000

'I see you've brought the English weather with you!' If I had a dollar for every time an American birder said those words to me last month, I'd be a rich man. We were in Cape May, New Jersey, enjoying the delights of spring migration, US-style.

The organisers of the Spring Birding Weekend were understandably miffed. After a heatwave earlier in the month, temperatures had plummeted, and clouds and rain were the order of the day. Because I am English, and was scheduled to give a talk on birds and weather, it was clearly all my fault. Not that the birds minded too much. True, it wasn't quite the spectacle we had been promised, but there was still plenty to keep us happy, with something new to see every day.

The only problem was what to call the birds we saw. When European settlers originally colonised North America, they were quite understandably homesick. So when they saw a vaguely familiar bird, they named it after one from back home. The trouble is that they were not all that good at identification.

This may explain why they have a robin the size of a thrush that looks like a blackbird. Sparrows that are actually buntings. And warblers. Not the drab, confusing mob we know and love, but a band of multicoloured, dancing sprites, which bring joy to even the most jaded birder, whatever the weather.

Then there is another confusing category: species which occur on both sides of the Atlantic, but have different names. When a birder called out 'Common Loon', on an otherwise uneventful offshore boat trip, he momentarily confused me. Lifting my binoculars, I realised I was looking at a Great Northern Diver in full breeding plumage. We were also hoping to see Parasitic Jaegers or, as we call them, Arctic Skuas. And I kept having to stop myself referring to waders, which over there are known as shorebirds.

For a while, the rain threatened to spoil the whole weekend. But as often happens with birding, an unpromising day can turn out much better than expected. As we were walking around the lake, with a group of beginner birders led by local expert Richard Crossley, we became aware of hundreds of birds swooping low over the water.

They were swallows, busily catching insects forced down by the poor weather. Not just one or two species, as we might expect in Britain, but no fewer than six different kinds. Once again, linguistic differences caused confusion when I called out Sand Martin (which they call Bank Swallow). By far the commonest species was the Barn Swallow, the same species we see every summer. But unlike our birds, these had rich russet underparts, rather than pale buff.

We could also see Tree Swallows, flashing bluish-green as they swooped before our eyes; Rough-winged Swallows, a chunkier version of the Sand Martin; huge, dark Purple Martins; and two Cliff Swallows, their pinkish rumps clearly visible as they flew by.

Despite this spectacular aerial display, our novice birders seemed singularly unimpressed. Richard, with classic Yorkshire tact, explained that this really was an unusual and impressive sight. Then we got to the bottom of the problem: the fact that to a beginner, all swallows look the same. So as the birds lined up conveniently on a telegraph wire, Richard pointed out their diagnostic features as patiently as he could. Under his expert tuition, people finally began to understand the subtle differences between the species, and frowns gave way to smiles.

Half an hour later, we reached the car park, soaked but satisfied. As we parted company, I wondered if one day in the future, those new birders will look back fondly on that damp afternoon as the first time they really began to appreciate the joys of birding – despite the weather.

Honeymoon in paradise

 NOVEMBER 2001

Suzanne and I left London mid-morning, on our honeymoon at last. By late afternoon we were sitting by the hotel pool sipping a cold beer and watching birds hop around the carefully manicured gardens. We might have been on the Isles of Scilly, Tenerife or Mallorca, but we weren't. It was nudging 100 degrees in the shade, the birds were new and exotic, and we were on another continent: Africa.

Our destination was The Gambia, that tiny West African republic just a six-hour flight from Gatwick. With only an hour's time difference, we didn't have to worry about jetlag, and we spent one of the most restful and stress-free fortnights I have ever experienced.

We also, I have to confess, went birding. OK, so watching birds isn't what you would call a traditional honeymoon activity, but birding is so easy in The Gambia that you can't really avoid it. Fortunately, too, Suzanne shares my enthusiasm and interest.

On our first evening, without leaving the poolside bar, we saw a Red-eyed Dove, Speckled Pigeon and the aptly named Beautiful Sunbird. On a quick walk around the Hotel Kairaba gardens we saw three species of glossy starling and two local specialities: White-crowned Robin-chat and Yellow-crowned Gonolek. These normally shy forest birds have become accustomed to people and perched invitingly close, allowing us to admire their splendid plumage.

The next day, in the grounds of the hotel next door, the Senegambia, we added even more species to our 'garden list'. These included shrikes, parrots and two species of kingfisher: the large, showy Blue-breasted, and the tiny, jewel-like African Pygmy Kingfisher, one of the highlights of the trip.

You could spend a fortnight here without leaving the hotel grounds, and you would still see more than 60 different species, while a couple of excursions on foot to the nearby rice fields, creek and forest would add another 50. So one morning we took a walk around Kotu Creek, where Pied Kingfishers hovered over the water, while flocks of Little Bee-eaters gathered nearby. We also saw male Red Bishops, looking like giant red-and-black bumblebees, perform their extraordinary display flight.

That evening, we explored Bijilo Forest Park, a tract of original palm forest just a few minutes walk from the hotel gates. At first, we saw very little, but as the sun began to set Swallow-tailed and Little Bee-eaters treated us to stunning close-up views. A perched raptor turned out to be a Lizard Buzzard, which stayed put long enough for us to admire its beautifully marked plumage through our new telescope.

But it was at dusk, as we strolled back towards the park gates, that we enjoyed the most memorable encounter, when three tiny, bantam-like birds appeared on the path a few metres ahead of us. They were Stone Partridges, a shy and elusive gamebird that rarely ventures out of the dense undergrowth. To our delight, the partridges carried on walking along the path, uttering quiet, liquid calls as they went, and allowing us to see every detail of their intricately marked plumage.

We wandered back along the beach, watching the sun set over the Atlantic, before enjoying a celebratory cocktail at the poolside bar. A notice proclaimed that it was happy hour. I couldn't argue with that.

Encounter with a Wanderer

 MARCH 2002

It all happened while I was eating my breakfast. I had just sat down to a nice plate of bacon and eggs when I caught sight of a huge bird as it glided past the window. Ignoring the rapidly congealing fry-up, I rushed outside to see this magnificent seabird in its full glory, an 11-foot wingspan enabling it to fly effortlessly above the waves. I had finally fulfilled my ambition to see a Wandering Albatross.

I was a long way from home: on a Russian icebreaker, at roughly 65 degrees west and 60 degrees south, on my way to Antarctica. The night before, we had set sail from the Argentinian city of Ushuaia. After a rocky night's sleep, we had awoken to a clear, bright morning on the open ocean.

This was not the first albatross I had seen. The previous afternoon, as we boarded the *Kapitan Dranitsyn*, I was gazing idly out into the harbour when I saw a black-and-white bird gliding on stiff wings in the far distance. It was a Black-browed Albatross, the wanderer's smaller cousin (although when comparing albatrosses, small is a relative term).

As we sailed through the Beagle Channel I saw plenty more Black-brows, with up to 50 circling the ship at any one time. I also saw my first penguin: a young Magellanic, looking like a lost duck as it swam along in front of the bow. As soon as the ship got too close, it disappeared beneath the surface of the water.

Within a couple of days I had enjoyed my fill of both penguins and albatrosses. In the South Shetlands we visited several colonies of Gentoo and Chinstrap Penguins, marvelling at the noisy spectacle of these delightful birds. Later, as we headed further south, we came across little groups of Adélie Penguins perched on ice floes, fleeing in panic as we crunched through the ice towards them.

The highlight, ornithologically speaking, was a single Emperor Penguin, sighted as we crossed Marguerite Bay. At first it was just a distant black-and-white speck, but as we approached it transformed into a magnificent specimen of the world's largest penguin species. These incredible birds are the archetypal Antarctic creature, spending virtually their whole life on the ice sheet.

But ultimately, it was neither the Wandering Albatross nor the Emperor Penguin that has stayed with me the longest. Nor was it the frequent encounters with seals and whales. It was the place itself: a constantly changing panorama of ice and snow, with more shades of white – and blue – than you can begin to imagine. A place unlike anywhere else on the planet: a virgin wilderness where the usual state of affairs is reversed, and you feel like an alien life-form visiting the Earth. A place where the silence is only broken by the hum of the ship's engines and the crack of breaking ice.

An early start in BA

APRIL 2002

We had sailed for two days and two nights across the southern oceans, followed by a four-hour flight to Buenos Aires, and a late night out in the Argentinian capital. So at two o'clock in the morning, as I sank into the comfort of my hotel bed, you might think I would have been looking forward to a lie-in. Instead, like any self-respecting birder, I set the alarm for 6 a.m.

When there are birds to be seen, an early start is essential. Even more so when the taxi to the airport is booked for midday. Fortunately my hotel, the Buenos Aires Hilton, was a mere stone's throw away from one of the best urban bird reserves in the world, Costanera Sur. Located alongside the Rio de la Plata, in the heart of a city of three million people, Costanera Sur is a patch of green amidst a sea of concrete – its reedbeds and lagoons acting as a magnet for breeding and migrating birds.

As a newcomer to South American birding, I had done my homework, checking out the species seen by a birding friend when he visited the reserve a few years ago. Even as I approached I could see flocks of Picazuro Pigeons flying overhead and hear the harsh calls of Monk Parakeets. Alongside the road was a thrush-sized bird with a reddish tail, which I identified as a Rufous Hornero (the first of many birds with extremely silly names).

I reached the reserve at ten minutes to seven, only to discover that it does not open until eight. Fortunately the road overlooks a long lagoon, which was simply packed with birds, including Wattled Jacanas, Snowy Egrets and the first of three different kinds of coot. A bizarre black-and-white bird with a long tail flew past: a Guira Cuckoo. And in the reedbed was a Masked Yellowthroat, with a song that reminded me of a cheerful Willow Warbler.

A patient wait paid off, with brief but excellent views of a Plumbeous Rail and Wren-like Rushbird, a diminutive little creature flicking in and out of the reeds. All this before I had even entered the reserve. When I finally did so, I was almost overwhelmed with the array of birds on offer. New species of grebes, ducks and swans; a stunning Fork-tailed Flycatcher; and a Glittering-breasted Emerald, a type of hummingbird which moved up and down the path so fast I could hardly focus my binoculars.

By now the temperature was starting to rise, and I was sharing the path with an army of joggers and cyclists. I was also struggling to put a firm identity to some of the new birds I saw. First, a huge finch-like bird with a bright orange bill, singing from the top of a stem of pampas grass: Great Pampa-finch. Then a black bird with a striking white mask around the eye: Spectacled Tyrant. And a thrush-like bird with a white stripe above the eye: Chalk-browed Mockingbird. One by one I worked my way through the various birds on offer, checking them out and ticking them off.

The sun continued to rise, and my time in this birder's paradise was fast running out. A last look round, then a swift walk back to the hotel, and the start of a long journey home. And the prize for the bird with the silliest name? It goes to a small bird with a truly magnificent moniker: the Many-coloured Rush-tyrant.

Swedish capers

 MAY 2002

Every birdwatcher has his or her 'bogey bird' – a species that despite years, even decades of trying, they have never seen. Occasionally you share your bogey bird with a fellow enthusiast, which explains how Bill Oddie and I came to be spending a night, last month, in a small hut in the middle of Sweden. Our quest was to see, after a total of almost a century of birding experience between us, a male Capercaillie.

You might not think that Capercaillies are a particularly difficult bird to find. After all, males are the size of a turkey, and spend spring mornings strutting around the forest floor displaying to each other. Indeed, compared to females, males of this species are so huge that a paper in an eminent ornithological journal once posed the rather dubious question: 'Why are Capercaillie cocks so big?'

Its name is also a bit of a puzzle. Derived from the Gaelic, is has been interpreted as meaning either 'old man', 'horse' or 'goat' of the woods. Whatever its derivation, over the years both Bill and I have been heard referring to it in less polite terms because despite many visits to its British stronghold, Speyside, we have never seen one. One reason is that Capercaillies are now very rare birds in Britain, due to a combination of shooting, collisions with deer fences and cold weather during the breeding season, which means many chicks die of exposure.

Every now and then, you hear of a rogue male Capercaillie, which instead of displaying to his fellow cocks, decides to threaten human visitors instead. Several television wildlife presenters, including Simon King and the great Sir David Attenborough, have been attacked on camera, but not, alas, the small bearded gentleman I work with. Perhaps they think he wouldn't put up much of a fight.

So, back to a long night in a Swedish pine forest. Our companions had left us there at 8 p.m., with strict warnings not to make a noise or emerge from the hut for at least 12 hours. When I say hut, I am stretching the point a little: a better word would be shed. Fortunately the excitement at the prospect of finally catching up with our quarry overrode any thoughts of comfort, so we squeezed inside and settled down to a night of fitful sleep.

Before we could doze off, however, we heard a loud rustle in the trees behind us. Carefully opening a tiny wooden observation slit, we gazed outside. At first, we saw nothing, but then, as we scanned upwards, there he was – an unmistakable, silhouetted shape. 'Can we go home now?' asked Bill. But we had clear instructions not to move, and besides, we had no idea where we were. So, tired but happy, we went to bed.

Dawn broke fitfully through the pine canopy, and with it, a most extraordinary sound: a rapidly accelerating series of echoing notes followed by what appeared to be a champagne cork being released. On the far horizon, two Capercaillie cocks were strutting their stuff.

We watched, entranced, for an hour or so, willing them to come closer as they spread their tail-feathers and performed their extraordinary mating dance. Unfortunately, they did not, and as the grey light of morning flooded the forest, they eventually disappeared. I have spent more comfortable nights birding, but rarely such a memorable one.

I say, I say: my wife went to the West Indies . . .

 **FEBRUARY 2003**

Jamaica is an excellent location for a winter birding trip – though you might not automatically associate the island with birds. One of my favourite bird families – the North American wood-warblers – has at least a dozen representatives wintering there, and almost every patch of trees contains at least one of these elegant, brightly coloured birds hawking for insects.

American Redstarts and Black-throated Blue Warblers were everywhere, while two other species – Cape May and Worm-eating Warblers – were new for me. The latter failed to live up to its name, foraging instead for insects high in the forest canopy. Another 'American' bird, the American Kestrel, was also common – either being mobbed by the ubiquitous Loggerhead Kingbird, or in turn chasing off the larger Red-tailed Hawk.

But the real attraction for visiting birders is the 28 endemic species – birds found nowhere else in the world. Jamaica has the highest number of endemics for any island its size – even more than neighbouring Cuba, an island ten times bigger. This is because of Jamaica's origin as an oceanic island, which has never been connected to any other landmass.

Several of the endemics are among the commonest birds, so from the first morning we enjoyed views of two delightful hummingbirds: the Red-billed Streamertail and the Jamaican Mango – both as beautiful as their names suggest. We also watched the antics of a pair of Vervain Hummingbirds. At less than two-and-a-half inches long, and weighing just three grams, this is the second smallest bird in the world (the even tinier Bee Hummingbird lives on Cuba). They look more like large flying insects than birds, and they buzz around from flower to flower like bumblebees, sipping nectar as they go.

Other endemic birds were much harder to find, requiring long treks into the famous coffee-growing area of the Blue Mountains; while we could bird at a more leisurely pace in the grounds of Hotel Mockingbird Hill, overlooking the resort of Port Antonio, on the north-east coast. Here, we saw both native species of cuckoo – the huge Chestnut-bellied and the smaller Jamaican Lizard-cuckoo. These are known as Old Man Bird and Old Woman Bird because their extraordinary calls sound like grumbling senior citizens!

Mockingbird Hill is also home to the island's newest endemic species, the Black-billed Streamertail. This elegant hummingbird has recently been given full specific status, as its song, habits and plumage all differ from those of its commoner relative, Red-billed Streamertail. Both are known locally as 'doctor bird', because their long tails resemble the tail-coats once worn by medical men.

On our final afternoon, we visited Rocklands bird-feeding station, near Montego Bay airport. Here, Red-billed Streamertails and Jamaican Mangos took sugar solution from a feeder – but this time perching on our fingers to do so.

Edge of the Arctic

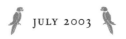

JULY 2003

The ferry journey lasted a shade under two hours, but took us back many years in time, to the little island of Flatey. Situated in a fjord which makes a major dent into Iceland's west coast, Flatey is home to two Eider farmers, a handful of summer holidaymakers and some of the loveliest birds I've ever seen.

As we got off the ferry, Puffins and Black Guillemots were bobbing up and down by the quayside – the latter in their smart black-and-white dress. This delightful auk is known locally as 'teista' – close enough to the Shetland word 'tystie' to reveal the common linguistic heritage between the two places.

In Britain you have to venture to the very highest tops of the Cairngorms to encounter breeding Snow Buntings, but here on Flatey they have become a garden bird. Lena, the Eider farmer's wife, regularly throws out home-baked bread and cakes for the buntings, which appeared to appreciate them as much as a hungry BBC camera crew did.

Another culinary treat on Lena's well-stocked dining table was Eider eggs. Served warm, these tasted fresher than any I have ever eaten – probably because the nests from which they had been collected were only a few minutes away. Haffstein, Lena's husband, collects the Eider's soft down, too – which fetches a premium price from Japanese buyers keen to get the perfect night's sleep.

After elevenses, lunch and afternoon tea we were ready to do some work, so we went in search of Flatey's two star species. Both are members of the phalarope family – a word derived from the Greek meaning 'coot foot', which refers to their partly webbed toes. For unlike other waders, phalaropes spend much of their time swimming, propelling themselves along like a child's clockwork toy.

Their other claim to fame is that the females are not only more colourful than the males, but take the initiative in courtship, too. Having laid their eggs, they leave the dowdier male to brood the clutch and look after the tiny chicks.

The commoner species of the two was the Red-necked Phalarope, with up to a dozen females congregating to bathe and squabble on the village pond each evening. With their steel-grey plumage and bright orange collars, they are a very handsome bird indeed.

But not quite as handsome as their cousin – the Grey Phalarope. If any bird has a really misleading name, then this one does. It's true that in autumn, when they occasionally appear in Britain on their way south, they are predominantly grey and white. But here on Flatey, at the very southern edge of their Arctic breeding range, they truly deserve their North American name of Red Phalarope.

Haffstein rowed us across to a tiny offshore island, in the company of Iceland's top ornithologist Dr Aevar Petersen. As the little boat approached the shore, we caught sight of what looked like two orange rugby balls floating in the seaweed. Phalaropes are notoriously tame, and they eventually allowed us to get within a few feet of them. Later on, we watched the sun finally dip beneath the horizon – a few minutes after midnight!

The youngest island

SEPTEMBER 2003

What was going on in November 1963? The Beatles were top of the hit parade, the Macmillan government was still reeling over the Profumo Affair and, in Dallas, President Kennedy was cruelly assassinated. Meanwhile, off the south coast of Iceland, a new island was emerging from the depths of the ocean.

Forty years later, historians continue to argue over the long-term impact of the events of that era. But the island of Surtsey – named after the Norse God of Fire, Surtir – is still there for us to marvel at and for a lucky few to visit. In June, I hitched a helicopter ride from the Icelandic coastguard, and fulfilled one of my lifetime ambitions: to set foot on a piece of land which did not even exist at the time of my birth.

I was afraid that the reality would not live up to my expectations, but I need not have worried. Surtsey is, quite simply, incredible: a lump of volcanic rock and ash, still bearing the scars of its extraordinary origins – the result of the eruption of an undersea volcano. From the air, shades of black and grey are relieved only by a single, dazzling patch of green.

As the sound of the helicopter drifted away towards the horizon, I looked up to see a Swallow hawking for insects over the black rocks. Swallows do not breed in Iceland, and this lone bird must have taken a diversion on its way from Africa to Scandinavia. As the sun shone, I wondered if it might decide to hang around until a mate arrived.

The next signs of life I saw were tiny plants, seemingly dropped directly onto the ashy 'soil'. Right from the start, Surtsey has been a living laboratory, enabling scientists to observe at first hand how life colonises a new environment. The first life-forms here were midges, closely followed by plants whose seeds had washed up on the shore. Today, parts of the island are quite well vegetated, thanks to a group of visitors I could no longer ignore: the gulls.

Gulls are among the most adaptable of birds, and although they were not the very first avian visitors here (that honour is shared by the Black Guillemot and Fulmar), they have certainly been the most successful. The green patch I could see from the helicopter is the site of the gull colony, and its verdant colour is a result of the birds returning to the mainland to feed, picking up seeds and then depositing them on Surtsey via their droppings. Once the seeds germinate they are fertilised by the gulls' guano, so that this part of the island resembles a rather bumpy lawn.

The feeling of being on the edge of Creation is accentuated by the noisy cries of the gulls as they defend their territories against incursion from their rivals. As I was watching them, I saw the Swallow again, taking advantage of the sun on its back to feed on the concentration of small flying insects attracted by the gulls.

After just two hours – far too short a time to explore this amazing place – the arrival of the helicopter signalled that my stay on Surtsey was over. The stay was so brief that it almost seemed like a dream – but in a way that is appropriate for an island that has only existed for 40 years.

The big one

OCTOBER 2003

I have a love–hate relationship with seabirds. I love them for their grace and beauty, and for their ability to survive in one of the world's harshest habitats. But I hate the agonies you have to go through to see them, especially seasickness.

From time to time, my desire to see these wonderful birds in their natural habitat overcomes my fears. So this autumn I went not once, but twice, on the best-known seabird-watching trip of all: off the coast of Monterey in northern California. It was led by the legendary Debra Love Shearwater, who is so obsessed by seabirds she changed her name to one!

Unlike the usual British experience, which involves long periods staring at an empty sea, we saw birds from the very start. Black Turnstones on the sea wall, Pigeon Guillemots in the harbour, and great rafts of Sooty Shearwaters just offshore. This is because unlike most coastal areas, Monterey is on the edge of a huge underwater canyon, with continual upwellings of cool water mixing with warm on the surface. This provides a perfect place for fish and other undersea creatures to thrive, in turn attracting thousands of seabirds from far and wide.

And I do mean far and wide: Buller's Shearwaters travel from New Zealand, Pink-footed Shearwaters from Chile and Black-footed Albatrosses all the way from Hawaii. These majestic birds spend up to a fortnight flying to Monterey, where they stock up on food, before returning to feed their very hungry chicks.

Pelagics can be very hit or miss, but for a change I was in luck: my first trip, in mid-September, was the best of the year. We saw five species of shearwater, three different jaegers (skuas to you and me), and four different kinds of storm-petrel, fluttering over the waves like marine versions of a House Martin. All this, on seas as calm as a millpond.

So when we assembled for the second trip, in early October, I was worried that it would not live up to expectations – especially as we were filming this time. Birdwise, it was not quite as good, as the huge shearwater flocks had departed, and despite extensive searching, we could not locate the storm-petrels. But what it may have lacked in birds, it made up for with marine mammals. Risso's and Pacific White-sided

Dolphins rode the bows, while Humpback Whales appeared in the distance.

Then came the big one, in every sense. On the far horizon, what looked like a fire hydrant went off, then another, closer spurt. Over the intercom, Debra uttered the words: 'We've got a Blue Whale!' We held our breath as the whale did the same, and watched as it emerged momentarily above the waves. Then, as we waited for another sighting, what appeared to be a small island surfaced right beside us: a smooth lump of grey, like a rock exposed by the receding tide.

The whale was there for a moment or two, before disappearing beneath the waves. It was a moment of pure magic. Ever since I first visited the Natural History Museum as a child and saw the life-size model of the Blue Whale, I had wanted to see the largest creature to have existed on Earth.

Dawn in the desert

 APRIL 2004

Dawn in the Sahara may sound romantic, but the reality was a chilly wind and temperatures more like England than Africa. Nevertheless, we set out early in search of one of Morocco's most elusive birds, the African Desert Warbler. It was a quest which seemed likely to fail, with the stiff breeze keeping activity to a minimum. But after persistent searching, the bird finally performed, perching on top of a tiny bush to sing its scratchy but tuneful song.

I was on a tour of southern Morocco with Limosa Holidays, and the north-west African target species were coming thick and fast. In equally unpromising weather we found Tristram's Warbler – similar in shape to a Dartford Warbler and named after Henry Baker Tristram, a Victorian country vicar who discovered the species while collecting birds in nearby Algeria. Later on we saw Egyptian and Red-necked

Nightjars, Fulvous Babblers and, rarest of all, the Northern Bald Ibis – of which only a few hundred individuals survive in the wild, virtually all in Morocco.

This particular day we were on an expedition to look for the species which every visiting birder hopes to see: Desert Sparrow. As a close relative of our familiar House Sparrow, this is not a bird to set the pulses of non-birders racing. But for the connoisseur, it is a real prize.

We had ditched our usual minibus for a trio of Land Rovers and set off down the bumpy track like competitors in the Paris–Dakar rally. Deserts are not noted for their abundance of birds, and we travelled several kilometres without seeing anything. Then the leading driver stopped and indicated the area in front of us. There, beautifully camouflaged against the sand and stones, stood a Cream-coloured Courser – one of the most elegant of all desert birds. Aware of our presence, it ran forward on its long legs, paused, and finally flew, revealing distinctive black underwings contrasting with its sandy coloured body.

Delighted with this unexpected sighting, we travelled on to the Café Yasmina, at an oasis on the edge of the Sahara. Oases act as a trap for migrants, and this one was no exception. Subalpine and Olivaceous Warblers, Black-eared Wheatears and a Rufous Bush Robin foraged among the trees, while both European and Blue-cheeked Bee-eaters hawked for insects overhead. The latter is one of the most beautiful birds in the world – but we dedicated sparrow searchers would not be sidetracked from our task.

Then a small, pale bird flew up into a tree and delivered a chirpy little song. It was our first Desert Sparrow – a fine male. Sighs of relief all round. We then set off for a nearby lake – the temporary result of recent rainfall. Here Black-winged Stilts, Ruddy Shelduck and Greater Flamingos were all taking advantage of this sudden gift from the heavens.

Time to return to our hotel, but not before our sharp-eyed driver found a pair of Desert Sparrows nesting in a lone palm tree. Cue a

frenzy of photography, led by David Cottridge, one of Britain's leading bird photographers, and our co-leader, Dutch ornithologist
Arnoud van den Berg.

Top garden birding

 NOVEMBER 2004

British birdwatchers abroad are sometimes accused of being so single-
minded in their pursuit of birds that they fail to notice the cultural
wonders of the places they visit. Likewise, watching birds on an organised tour can insulate you from the very people through whose land
you are passing. But sometimes you just can't help noticing something
other than birds: as I discovered earlier this month on a visit to Iguazu,
on the border between Argentina, Brazil and Paraguay.

For a start, there are the famous Iguazu waterfalls themselves. Rated
by many as one of the seven natural wonders of the world, the volume
of water passing through the cataracts is unbelievable. Even so, I was
momentarily distracted by flocks of Great Dusky Swifts, which literally fly through the streams of water, in order to reach their nests
behind. Presumably they do so to avoid attack by predators, but their
lifestyle choice brings other hazards: the morning after a cloudburst the
extra rush of water appeared to have swept most of the nests away.

The rainforests around the falls are equally productive for birds,
though as in all jungle habitats to see anything you need a combination
of patience, luck and an ability to resist the attentions of mosquitoes.
Our first walk, in the late afternoon, was fairly unproductive, although
as ever we heard all sorts of intriguing sounds from birds we could not
see.

Several dawn starts, especially when accompanied by Daniel, our
expert local guide, were much more productive. We saw three species
of toucan, including the huge version made famous by Guinness

adverts; two trogons (one of which materialised out of nowhere in response to a tape recording of its song); and many other forest birds, including colourful tanagers, a tiny woodpecker-like piculet, and the extraordinary White-bearded Manakin, the males of which attract their mates by loudly clicking their wings.

But for an event which combined the very best of South American birding with a truly rewarding cultural experience, my colleague Mike and I travelled into the local town of Puerto Iguazu. There, we visited the Jardin de Picaflores – the garden of hummingbirds – owned by a local couple who have dedicated their lives to showing the beauty of these gorgeous birds to anyone who cares to visit.

Even before we could sit down we were assailed from all sides by the whirring of tiny wings. Just a few feet in front of us, plastic feeders filled with nectar were being visited by a constant stream of different birds, each of which hovered momentarily to feed, then flew off like a bullet.

Hummingbird identification is never easy: the birds rarely stick around for very long, and the males and females of each species are often very different in appearance. But we took a deep breath, and with the expert help of the owners we gradually began to get our eye in.

An hour later, we had managed to identify no fewer than eight different species, including the iridescent Glittering-bellied Emerald, the splendid Black Jacobin, and the enormous (at least for a hummingbird!) Scale-throated Hermit. All the while, we had been joined by a procession of local mums, dads and children, all highly entertained at watching two slightly mad British birders having the time of their lives.

CHAPTER 6

Birds, places and people

I n some ways, this chapter is a miscellany of odds and ends: pieces that don't quite fit into neat categories elsewhere. But it has its own coherence: the same themes recur at different times, reflecting my continuing obsessions.

In no particular order, these are:

- birds I have seen – often triggered by a single sighting that in some way revealed something new in my mind about a familiar species;
- birds I have yet to see – a very long list, for which I selected my top eight for a piece loosely based on *Desert Island Discs*;
- people I have met – especially those involved in the development of birdwatching from a minority hobby into a global pastime, such as the late Max Nicholson;

- birding with friends – the often underrated social aspect of birding, and the wider benefits the pastime has for our emotional and spiritual lives;
- birds I love – all of them, really; but in particular my favourite bird of all, the Swift.

What only occurred to me as I was compiling this book were the extraordinary changes that have occurred in such a short time – not much more than a decade since I wrote my very first *Guardian* column (the piece on gulls that opens this chapter).

For example, in 1993 I wrote about gulls' habit of wintering inland; today we have tens of thousands of pairs breeding inland, too, on the roofs of our major cities. When I first wrote this column, if you wanted to see Red Kites you had to travel to mid-Wales; today, thanks to a successful reintroduction programme, they are a common sight in many parts of the country. And who could have foreseen that for a period we would be forced to avoid some of our favourite corners of the countryside as a result of foot-and-mouth disease?

Finally, several of the pieces in this chapter reflect on the wider meaning of birding – not just why we do it, but why we *need* to do it; why, in essence, watching and enjoying birds is good for us.

The joy of gulls

 JANUARY 1993

At first sight, gulls don't have a lot going for them. Compared with the beauty of Kingfishers, the grace of Avocets or the splendour of Golden Eagles, it's no wonder that, for many people, they are low down the bird-appreciation hit parade.

But gulls have something else in their favour – something pretty useful in today's world. They're successful. No other group of species is quite so well adapted to late twentieth-century life – a life lived alongside all the effluents, pollutants and rubbish produced by humans. Gulls are a kind of avian waste-disposal system. Especially during the winter months, great flocks of them gather at rubbish tips and sewage outfalls – anywhere there's something to eat.

Gulls appearing inland in winter is a relatively recent phenomenon, and numbers have increased dramatically since the Second World War. Indeed as recently as 1945 the Black-headed Gull was described as an 'uncommon visitor' to the London area. Today, this species spends virtually all its life away from the coast, so the word 'seagull' is becoming less and less appropriate.

During the short daylight hours, gulls' main concern is finding food. Being more or less omnivorous, they find waste-disposal sites most to their liking. Almost any edible refuse, from carcasses to vegetable peelings and chicken bones to excrement, will eventually find its way down their ever-open gullets. In recent years the sheer numbers of these flocks – anything up to 50,000 birds at a single site – has caused problems. Many of these are associated with the gulls' habit of communal roosting during the night.

Gulls are creatures of habit. Every evening, an hour or so before dusk, they begin to leave their feeding grounds and head towards a roosting site – usually a large area of water such as a reservoir. The health hazard of thousands of gulls defecating into the water supply is truly mind-boggling. But in west London, roosting gulls present an even greater danger. The gulls' own flight-path, from Poyle rubbish tip, near Staines, to the nearby Queen Mary Reservoir, passes right across the busiest man-made flight-path in the world – the main runway in and out of Heathrow Airport.

But not all our gulls spend the winter inland. Despite Britain's dwindling fishing fleet, ports and harbours are still a good place to find the more marine species. The archetypal 'seagull', the Herring Gull, predominates, usually accompanied by its larger cousin, the predatory Great Black-backed Gull.

For the sharp-eyed birdwatcher, there are more unusual visitors to be found among the gull flocks. A Ring-billed Gull from North America is currently spending its fifth successive winter on a recreation ground in Uxbridge, Middlesex. And as many as 50 Mediterranean Gulls have taken up winter residence at the sewage outfall at Copt Point, Folkestone.

Hundreds of miles to the north, at Scottish fishing ports such as Ullapool and Stornoway, two refugees from the Arctic can be found. Glaucous and Iceland Gulls can be told apart from their commoner relatives by their all-white wing-tips, giving them a ghostly appearance in the fading afternoon light, as they follow the fishing fleet home.

This winter, the eastern Scottish port of Fraserburgh has played host to an even rarer Arctic wanderer, the legendary Ross's Gull. This tiny bird, less than half the size of its larger relatives, has a plumage tinged pink by its main diet – shrimps from the Arctic Ocean.

After breeding in the remotest corners of Siberia, Ross's Gull normally spends the winter around the Arctic Circle – one of the most northerly winter ranges of any bird. But for at least three wandering individuals, the lure of the fish-offal of Fraserburgh has finally proved too strong.

Flight of the skuas

 MAY 1993

Aird an Runair is, as Private Frazer of *Dad's Army* might have said, 'a wild and lonely place'. On the north-western edge of the island of North Uist, in the Outer Hebrides, nothing but the Atlantic Ocean separates it from North America. This makes it the perfect spot to watch the British weather approaching from the west, the clouds rushing in from the sea like film that has been speeded-up.

One May during the 1970s, a Kentish birdwatcher, David Davenport, made the long journey to North Uist, on a specific quest. Spring is the perfect time to visit the Western Isles: tiny flowers carpet the meadows, breeding Lapwings perform tumbling flights over the machair, and if you're lucky, a splendid Golden Eagle may soar into view. Most prized of all, the elusive and mysterious Corncrake, returned from its African winter-quarters, keeps islanders and visitors awake all night with its repetitive call.

But Davenport had other things in mind: having looked at the weather maps, and studied seabird migration routes, he was convinced that he would discover one of the most extraordinary avian spectacles in the British Isles – the passage flight of skuas past the Hebridean coast.

Skuas are the hawks of the sea: the scourge of weaker seabirds such as terns and auks. They prowl around a seabird colony until they spot a bird which has just caught a fish. Then they pounce, swooping down on the unsuspecting victim and harassing it until it drops or regurgitates its catch.

Two species of skua breed in Britain: the Great Skua or Bonxie, and the smaller and more falcon-like Arctic Skua. Both nest on the moors of Scotland and the Atlantic islands. But two other species of skua also visit our shores from time to time. The bulky Pomarine and the slender, tern-like Long-tailed Skua are rare passage migrants, usually seen only briefly as they pass by our coasts in spring or autumn. Both breed in the high Arctic, sharing their nesting grounds with polar foxes and snow-white hares.

As David Davenport looked west from Aird an Runair that windy spring day, he must have been amazed at what he saw. Tight flocks of Pomarine Skuas flew over the waves in close formation, like a squadron of fighter planes. These birds, with their extraordinary twisted tail-feathers, were joined from time to time by delicate Long-tailed Skuas, many sporting the magnificent elongated tail plumes worn by breeding adults.

What brought these skuas so close to land were the weather conditions that day. A deep low pressure area, moving north past the islands, brought strong westerly winds, veering north-westerly. These had blown the skuas close inshore – so close that some passed directly over the beach.

Given suitable weather conditions, the Hebridean skua passage has been noted most years since. The record was set in mid-May 1991, when 622 Pomarines and an astonishing 1346 Long-tails flew north in a fortnight, shattering the previous record of 388 birds in May 1983. The greatest spectacle was on 19 May, when lucky observers logged 540 Long-tails and over 100 Pomarines.

But skua-watchers already packing their bags for the Hebrides may be disappointed. When the winds fail to blow from the right direction, a whole season can pass with hardly any sightings.

Goshawk quest

JULY 1993

A warm evening, somewhere in the west of England. Just a few yards from a forest path, a man carrying a rope, a ladder and a rucksack is preparing to climb an oak tree. No, he's not up to mischief, though at first sight you might well be suspicious. His mission is to find, catch and ring the young of Britain's most enigmatic bird of prey: the Goshawk.

Few birdwatchers have ever seen a wild Goshawk in this country, even though more than 200 pairs now breed here. For such a huge bird, the Goshawk is remarkably elusive. One reason is its secretive habits: it lives deep in our largest forests, rarely venturing beyond the confines of the trees. When it does, its huge size and powerful flight action distinguish it from its smaller relative, the Sparrowhawk.

Another reason is that the Goshawk is itself a hunted creature – by humans. Unscrupulous egg-collectors and falconers frequently raid nests, taking both eggs and young for profit. Hence the need for secrecy during my visit to one of the Goshawk's most successful strongholds, in the heart of a lowland forest.

The ringer was barely halfway up the tree when we glimpsed the largest chick raising her head above the rim of the nest. After the three young birds were brought down, they were duly ringed and weighed, while I heard the story of the species' colonisation of Britain.

Goshawks nested here until the mid-nineteenth century, when they were driven to extinction by a combination of deforestation, the gamekeeper's trap and the Victorian bird-collector's gun. Then, in the late 1960s, they were discovered breeding in several parts of the country. Given that many of these early colonisers wore falconers' jesses, it seems certain that most, if not all, were escaped birds.

In this particular forest, the first bird was seen by a teacher leading a school party in 1978. He returned the following year to find a nesting pair, from which today's healthy population has grown. Since then he and a dedicated group of watchers have monitored the fate of the birds, spending their spare time tracking down new nests each spring.

Goshawks prey mostly on crows, jays and pigeons, so they are not short of food. But their catholic diet isn't the only reason for their success. At a second nest, we found telltale feathers, barred brown and white – revealing that the hen bird was in her first season, unusual among birds of prey.

Well able to survive the vagaries of the British weather, and with large areas of potential habitat not yet colonised, there seems little reason why the Goshawk should not become fully established throughout Britain. Provided, of course, that secrecy is maintained. In other parts of the country, they've been prevented from establishing themselves by constant persecution. Thanks to the efforts of the people with me, this particular population has avoided that fate.

Deep in the forest, as the sun went down, the ringer placed the young Goshawks in his rucksack. After a swift ascent, they were safely back in the nest. Meanwhile the female flew overhead, occasionally visible through the forest canopy as she called in apprehension. But this time at least, her fears were groundless, and her haunting, repetitive call only a false alarm.

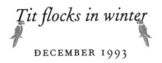

Tit flocks in winter

DECEMBER 1993

Visit a wood on a dull, grey winter's afternoon, and you could be forgiven for thinking no birds live there at all. There is no song, no movement, no sign of life. It's tempting to give it up as a bad job and to return home to the comforts of central heating and supper.

But wait. Was that a bird calling – at a pitch almost too high for the human ear? Perhaps it was just the wind . . . No – there it goes again: a thin, sibilant whistle, so quiet you have to turn your head this way and that to try to work out where it's coming from. Then, just as you think you must be mistaken, you hear another sound. Then another, and another – a whole chorus of off-key squeaks. After perhaps an hour of searching you've discovered the only birds in the whole wood – a roving flock of tits.

Or perhaps it's more accurate to say that they've discovered you. Keep still, don't make any sudden movements or noise, and they may pause for a moment in the bare branches above your head. Even then, they can be surprisingly difficult to see. The key is to fix your sights on any movement, carefully lift your binoculars to your eyes and focus. You may be lucky enough to catch a glimpse of a tiny bird, the owner of that high-pitched squeak, before it springs off to another branch and out of sight.

In winter, small birds need to eat about one quarter of their body weight every day – simply to survive. Their strategy depends on hunting in flocks for the few remaining grubs and insects lurking among the twigs and branches. A flock may consist of anything between ten and a hundred birds – mostly Blue Tits, with their striking blue-and-yellow plumage. These will usually be accompanied by Great Tits – larger, white-cheeked, black-capped and with a yellow breast.

Just as you're beginning to wonder whether anything more unusual is tagging along, a smaller bird flits across your field of view. More rounded, almost ball-like, and with a brown and black plumage, Coal Tits have left the dark coniferous forests where they breed to join their cousins in this broad-leaved woodland.

Tit flocks often attract one or two fellow-travellers: perhaps a Nuthatch or the small, brown, mouse-like Treecreeper. Our smallest bird, the Goldcrest, gives its presence away by its thin, high-pitched call as it flits from tree to tree. If you're really lucky (it's happened to me just once in many years of birding), you may even see a Lesser Spotted Woodpecker, hardly bigger than a sparrow, tagging along behind the flock.

Suddenly, you hear a new, three-note call, repeated by a chorus of birds. You glimpse what looks like a ball of fluff with a tail, shooting across the sky between the trees, followed in quick succession by two or three more. These are Long-tailed Tits, immortalised by the nine-teenth-century poet John Clare using a local name from his native Northamptonshire:

> And coy bumbarrels twenty in a drove
> Flit down the hedgerows in the frozen plain
> And hang on little twigs – and start again . . .

Still accompanied by an orchestra of calls, a flurry of activity fills the trees. Then, as quickly and suddenly as it appeared, the flock has gone – to some more productive area of the wood. By March, when the frozen ground is thawing, and the buds begin to sprout on the trees, perhaps one in five of these tiny birds will have survived. The rest lie in the leaf-litter, forever silent.

Birds over the Broads

MARCH 1994

There aren't many birds which have given their name to a piece of machinery. The crane is a notable exception. But the comparison fails to do justice to this magnificent species. Standing almost as tall as a grown man, with a long, curved neck and dagger-like bill, the crane fully deserves its reputation as the aristocrat of birds.

In medieval times, the crane was a dish fit for kings, when along with roast swan and stewed heron, it was served at royal banquets. The pressure from hunting, together with the draining of its native East Anglian fens, eventually took its toll, and by the year 1600 it was extinct as a British breeding species.

Since then, the crane has continued to survive on the Continent, though it has declined steadily, as its wetland habitats disappear. Cranes are shy birds, needing large areas of undisturbed land to breed. Today the species is mainly confined to the wet meadows, marshes and bogs of Scandinavia, where the returning birds perform their famous courtship dance each spring.

Each autumn, vast V-shaped flocks of cranes travel southwards, to spend the winter in the warmer climes of Spain, North Africa and the Middle East. En route, they run all kinds of risks: from the disappearance of feeding areas through habitat loss, to the shotguns of Mediterranean hunters.

Yet despite these problems, there is a small glimmer of hope for this splendid bird. For the past decade or so, a tiny population of cranes has bred in a remote corner of England – the Broadland area of north-east Norfolk. Despite their natural appearance, the Broads owe their existence to our ancestors' need to dig for peat to burn as fuel. Today, these reed-fringed lakes have become a holiday destination for thousands of pleasure-boat owners and day-trippers.

Yet even during the noise and bustle of the summer season, a few pairs of cranes have found an undisturbed spot to build their nests. Since 1981, they have raised at least four young, despite the ever-present threat from foxes, rats and, of course, humans.

For birds of their size, the Norfolk cranes have been remarkably successful at keeping out of sight. Their nesting-place remains a closely guarded secret, but during the winter months they can often be seen from the quiet road running along the coast. Their presence here during the winter is due to the relatively mild British climate, which enables them to forgo the risks of a long migration and to stay near their breeding grounds.

On a visit to Norfolk last month I came across the flock, now numbering nine birds, feeding along the edge of a ploughed field near the village of Waxham. With their elegant gait, steel-grey plumage and mass of curling tail-feathers, they looked more like Victorian ladies out for a Sunday-afternoon stroll than their mechanical namesake. They fed in a leisurely manner, bending their long necks to turn the soil in search of morsels of food to satisfy their omnivorous appetite.

It is hoped that eventually this small family flock might colonise other suitable areas and re-establish the crane as a British breeding bird. Stately and proud in the afternoon mist, the Norfolk cranes are true pioneers.

Millennium fever

 DECEMBER 1999

Millennium fever is upon us, and with it a glut of articles looking back over the past thousand years. My aim is more modest: to review some of the changes that have taken place in Britain's birdlife during the past century and to look ahead to what we can expect during the next.

At the start of the twentieth century, Britain's birdlife was, like the curate's egg, good in parts. Farmland birds generally thrived, benefiting from the gradual replacement of forests by agricultural land during the previous millennium. The birds of woodland, wetland, moor and mountain weren't too badly off either, for the Industrial Revolution hadn't affected most rural habitats.

But one group of birds was in big trouble: birds of prey. Almost any kind of hawk, buzzard or eagle was shot, trapped or poisoned, in some cases virtually out of existence. By 1900 Red Kites were down to a handful of pairs, and even these were subject to what Max Nicholson described as 'the Victorian leprosy of collecting'. Egg-collecting, known in pseudo-scientific circles as oology, had a very real effect on populations of rare breeding birds. It almost certainly hastened the extinction, in 1916, of our largest raptor, the magnificent White-tailed Eagle.

Later on in the twentieth century, raptors faced another hazard from pesticides such as DDT, which thinned their eggshells and led to catastrophic population declines. When I was growing up in south-west London during the 1970s, any bird of prey other than a Kestrel was a rare sight indeed.

Today, things are very different. Several species of raptor, including the Peregrine, Hobby and Sparrowhawk, are doing very well indeed. Others, such as the Red Kite, Osprey and Marsh Harrier, are still fairly localised, but much more common than they once were. I can still recall seeing Britain's last remaining pair of Marsh Harriers at Minsmere in 1973. Today there are more than a hundred pairs, breeding in suitable habitat all over southern Britain.

There have been other success stories, too, though some are less welcome than others. Introduced species, such as Canada Goose and Ruddy Duck, are doing very well in the absence of competitors, while native birds such as the Woodlark and Dartford Warbler are also thriving. Mild winters have helped the Wren displace the Blackbird and Chaffinch as our commonest bird, while the ample supply of food on waste-disposal sites has enabled several species of gull to spend the winter inland.

So what of the future? Have our farmland birds finally turned the corner, or will once widespread rural species such as the Corn Bunting and Yellowhammer continue their seemingly inevitable decline? Will seabirds such as the Arctic Tern and Kittiwake overcome food shortages, or will there be a sudden population collapse? Can the Red-backed Shrike and Wryneck come back from the brink and return to breed in our countryside?

In my view, by far the greatest threat facing our birdlife at the turn of the millennium is global warming. For some species, a warmer climate spells extinction, as habitats change irrevocably or disappear. For others, especially birds whose breeding ranges lie to the south, it offers an opportunity to colonise Britain and Ireland.

Early casualties are likely to include the Ptarmigan, whose arctic-alpine habitat looks set to disappear during the first half of the coming century. Others, such as the Snowy Owls that bred on Shetland during a spell of cooling during the 1960s and 1970s, have already gone.

At the other end of the country, birdwatchers have a more pleasing prospect to look forward to. Recent colonists such as the Little Egret and Cetti's Warbler will undoubtedly extend their ranges northwards, while future breeding species are likely to include Black Kite and Cattle Egret – both common on the near Continent. Meanwhile the aliens, such as Ring-necked Parakeet, should take advantage of mild winters and plentiful supplies of food to spread throughout southern Britain.

Bring me sunshine

MARCH 2000

Before the First World War, when my grandmother was growing up in Devon, she recalled her father saying that a bird was calling out his name. Of course it couldn't manage his full name – Edgar George

Russell Snow – so it settled for a less formal greeting: 'Snowy, Snowy, pay the rent, pay the rent!'

Almost a century later, even on this meagre evidence, I can identify the species my great-grandfather listened to all those years ago. That insistent, repetitive, rhythmic phrase could only belong to one bird: the Song Thrush.

Using a mnemonic to remember a particular call or song is one of the most enduring aspects of our long-standing relationship with birds. Even today, when I hear a Yellowhammer singing it's hard to resist calling back: 'A little bit of bread and no cheeeese!' Pied Wagtails (at least those living in London) call out 'Chis-ick'; and on spring evenings in the suburbs, thrushes tell little children to 'Go to bed! Go to bed!'

Other birds quite literally call out their own name. Cuckoo, Chiffchaff and Kittiwake are perhaps the best-known examples of onomatopoeic bird names. In the Cuckoo's case this goes back at least as far as the thirteenth century, when the bird made an appearance in one of the first poems written in modern English: 'Sumer is icumen in, Lhude sing, cuccu!'

Less obvious examples include the word finch. This comes from 'spink', a local Norfolk name for the Chaffinch – a reference to the bird's call. Many of the crow family also bear names derived from their harsh calls, including Rook, Jackdaw and Chough (originally pronounced 'chow', rather than 'chuff'). Many people assume that the name of our largest wader, the Curlew, refers to its decurved bill, but it actually comes from the bird's evocative call.

With bird songs and calls so deeply imprinted on our minds, it is hardly surprising that composers have taken advantage of our familiarity with these natural sounds. A recent report claimed that a Mozart composition was inspired by, of all unlikely sources, the sound of the Starling. During the twentieth century, the French composer Messiaen drew inspiration from a wide range of birds, including the fluty song of the Woodlark.

Nor is the traffic purely one-way. Starlings themselves are masters of mimicry, able to imitate car alarms, telephone bells and even snatches of song heard on a distant radio. Parrots, mynah birds and a whole host of other species have the ability to mimic pieces of classical and popular music.

Other birds have songs which bear an uncanny, though presumably unintentional, resemblance to well-known tunes. A recent correspondent to the *Guardian* letters page recalled hearing a bird singing the theme tune to the BBC's six o'clock news bulletin. But this was no case of slavish imitation – the bird and the listener were both thousands of miles away, in South Africa.

A couple of years ago, when I was in Kenya's Masai Mara, I had a similar experience. Each morning, as the sun rose over Governors' Paradise Camp, a bird would sing the first phrase of Morecambe and Wise's famous signature tune, *Bring Me Sunshine*. Each morning I would scan the forest canopy in the hope of catching a glimpse of this elusive songster, but without success.

After about a fortnight, I finally pinned down the bird, and was rather disappointed to find that it wasn't dressed in top hat and tails. With the help of a field guide, I identified it as a Chin-spot Batis, a tiny, tit-like songbird. Where this little black-and-white creature learnt to pay homage to Eric and Ernie, I never managed to discover.

Driving me crazy

 JULY 2000

Most birders keep lists. A British list, of all the birds they've seen in this country. A life list, of all the birds they've ever seen, anywhere in the world. And in my case, a journey to work list.

Depending which way you look at it, I am fortunate that my journey to work takes longer than most. Although I live in south London, I travel once a week to Bristol, a return trip of almost 300 miles. So I spend a lot of time on the road, and while Radio 4 staves off the boredom for a while, inevitably I turn to other means of amusement. Hence the list.

There are several drawbacks to birding while driving. First, because I obviously can't use binoculars, I don't see many small, hard-to-identify species. And if I really wanted to maximise my list, I could have picked a better route than the M25, M4 and M32. Britain's motorway system hardly ranks among the world's top birding hotspots, but even so, I do get a few surprises.

Take last Monday. There I was, stuck in a traffic jam on the M25 (what's new?), when a small, fast-flying bird whipped across the carriageway. I only saw it for a second or two, but its identity was never in doubt. A Kingfisher, doing its own spot of commuting from one gravel-pit to another and diverting my attention away from the traffic news for a moment.

Some birds are commonplace on motorways. Crows, Wood Pigeons and the ubiquitous Kestrels, hovering above the verge in search of their rodent prey. Sparrowhawks, too, though you have to be quick to notice them as they speed low past your windscreen. And more remarkably, Buzzards. I've often seen them on the western section of the M4, past Swindon. But one warm summer's evening, I noticed a pair of these majestic birds of prey loafing over the motorway near Maidenhead, barely 30 miles west of London.

Stops for rest and refreshment can be productive, too. Membury Services is home to the best coffee and croissants on the M4, consumed to the musical accompaniment of singing Skylarks. Pied Wagtails forage for crumbs in the car park, as do Rooks, as befits the rural surroundings. At the end of my journey, the entry to Bristol usually produces Herring and Lesser Black-backed Gulls, refugees from the nearby docks.

Sometimes I take a short diversion, driving through Hampton Court to drop my son David off at school. One frosty winter's day was particularly busy, with Long-tailed Tits, a Mandarin Duck and the usual flocks of parakeets screeching overhead. I am sometimes tempted to cheat and take an even longer route, but feel that the potential new species would hardly compensate for the horrors of a five-hour journey.

And the most unusual thing I've seen on my travels? Well, the Mandarin and Kingfisher come close, and I'm pretty sure I saw an Osprey once – but it was gone too quickly to be certain, and you can't really do a U-turn on the M4. In fact the best sighting of all came the same morning as the Kingfisher. Having escaped the M25, I was just getting used to the unfamiliar sensation of fifth gear, when a traffic jam forced me to slow down. A police car was trundling along the hard shoulder, presumably escorting a heavy load or broken-down motorist. Or so I thought.

But as we crawled past, the true nature of the policeman's errand became clear. Waddling along behind the panda car was a swan, accompanied by half-a-dozen cygnets, all enjoying the benefits of a VIP escort. I smiled all the way to work. Well, to the next traffic jam, at least.

Wetland wonderland

 AUGUST 2000

Back in the 1970s, when other kids were playing with their Chopper bikes and Spacehoppers, I had other things on my mind. And if I had to disobey the law to get what I wanted, so be it. Thus it was that early on a Sunday morning I could regularly be found 'breaking and entering' at an industrial site in south-west London. Fortunately, I rarely fell foul of the boys in blue, who obviously did not mind that a 13-year-old boy was climbing a fence to get into Barn Elms Reservoirs. After all, I could not really get up to much harm – apart from drowning, perhaps.

I was there, of course, to watch birds. And these four basins of water alongside the River Thames at Hammersmith provided birds aplenty. Ducks, with wintering Goldeneyes and Goosanders. Passing waders, such as Ruffs, Green Sandpipers and Little Ringed Plovers. And the chance of a real rarity, like the Desert Wheatear which arrived all the way from North Africa one warm spring day, and which I still managed to miss.

Today, the birds are still at Barn Elms. But apart from that, things have changed a bit. The site is now London's latest visitor attraction, with hordes of eager families walking along manicured paths, delighting in the variety of birds, insects and plants to be found there. It even has a new name: the London Wetland Centre.

The Wetland Centre was the brainchild of the twentieth century's greatest conservationist, Sir Peter Scott. Sadly he did not live to see the fulfilment of his dream, but if he had, I am sure he would have been overjoyed. The Wildfowl and Wetlands Trust (WWT) has transformed the derelict and disused reservoirs into a haven for wildlife, no distance from central London.

Funnily enough, the first thing that struck me was not the birds, but the richness of the habitat itself. WWT ecologists have lovingly re-created natural ponds and reedbeds by taking plants from elsewhere in the country and replanting them here. In turn, the plants have attracted an impressive array of insects, including dragonflies and damselflies. One of the highlights of my visit was close-up views of a huge Emperor dragonfly laying its eggs on the surface of the water.

I am no plant expert, but the variety of colours and textures managed to draw my attention away from the birds, at least momentarily. Purple loosestrife, reed-mace and flowering rush provided a stunning sight, glowing in the afternoon sun.

There were birds, too, of course: families of Coots and Moorhens, a surprisingly confiding Little Grebe, and flocks of Linnets and Goldfinches feeding on the banks of thistles or perched on the surrounding fence. Clouds of House Martins and Swifts decorated the sky, although the expected Hobby failed to materialise.

Further along the trail, there were displaying Ruddy Ducks in an area of open water, while Common Sandpipers and Little Ringed Plovers fed on the muddy edges. Lapwings breed, and Snipe and Kingfishers may soon do so – little short of a miracle this close to the heart of a major city.

Local birders have already found a few scarce visitors, with regular Avocets and the occasional passing Osprey or Red Kite. If and when a really rare bird turns up, families out for their Sunday afternoon stroll will undoubtedly find themselves surrounded by an invading army of twitchers.

Whether you are a keen birder or just a casual visitor, it is worth trying the café, whose food is a cut above the usual standard at bird reserves. A few years ago, the V&A ran a much-derided advertising campaign in a misguided attempt to attract the casual visitor. Maybe the Wetland Centre should market itself with a revised version: 'An ace caff with a very nice wetland attached'.

Desert Island Birds

 SEPTEMBER 2000

Anyone who has ever listened to Radio 4's longest-running programme, *Desert Island Discs*, has no doubt thought about which records, book and luxury item they would take with them to that imaginary isle. Birders can play a variation on the game: choosing a selection of birds which bring back memories of a lifetime's birding. Putting questions of practicality and habitat aside (would a Snowy Owl survive?), here are my eight desert island birds.

First, Coot, because without this humble waterbird I might never have taken up birdwatching. It was on a cold winter's day back in 1963, when my mother took me to feed the ducks on the River Thames. I saw some Coots, identified them using *The Observer's Book of Birds*, and was hooked.

Next, Great Crested Grebe: partly because it is such a beautiful bird, but mainly because it was the local speciality on the gravel-pits at Shepperton, where I grew up. I remember spending hours watching them, especially during the breeding season, when adults carried the humbug-striped young on their backs.

Third, another bird of my youth, Little Bittern. This is an elusive, reed-dwelling species of heron, which hardly ever shows itself, and is a rare vagrant to Britain. Its presence in my pantheon of all-time greats rests solely on the efforts of one wandering individual, which turned up at Stodmarsh in Kent in May 1975, when my teenage companions and I enjoyed brief but close-up views of this skulking beauty.

I did not get out birding much in the 1980s, mainly as a result of the demands of career and children. So I was always grateful to my fourth choice, the Swift, for reminding me that there was a world out there, beyond the city. Every May, regular as clockwork, screaming packs of Swifts would arrive in whatever part of London I was living, and tear across the sky like demons. Even today, I still await their arrival with a child-like eagerness, as they seem to sum up the hopes and dreams of the coming summer.

My fifth and sixth choices are birds which, in different ways, gave me memorable experiences while I was making the television series *Birding with Bill Oddie*. The first of these, Blue-cheeked Bee-eater, was a lost and lonely individual catching bumblebees in the unlikely setting of a Shetland garden. The other, Common Crane, was in northern Israel, where I watched thousands of these majestic birds flying into their winter roost at dusk, calling as they came. Simply unforgettable.

If I were to pick a desert island to spend the rest of my life, then it would be Little Tobago, which lies just off the coast of its larger neighbour. Little Tobago plays host to one of the world's finest seabird colonies, with boobies and frigatebirds soaring around its cliffs. It is also the home of my seventh choice, arguably the most beautiful bird in the world: Red-billed Tropicbird. Watching these angelic creatures waft through the air against a topaz-blue sky is a fabulous experience.

And my final choice? A bird that I had to travel to the ends of the Earth to see: Wandering Albatross. Tragically, like all the world's albatrosses, this magnificent seabird is in danger of extinction because of deaths caused by longline fishing in the southern oceans. Seeing it, as with any albatross, is a privilege.

Oh, I almost forgot. What about my book and luxury item? Choosing a single bird book from so many is tough, but for comprehensive coverage of birds on any desert island, and indeed everywhere else, I would have to pick the multi-volume *Handbook of the Birds of the World*. And my luxury item? Yes, you've guessed it: a pair of binoculars!

Return to the desert island

 FEBRUARY 2002

A little while ago, I devoted this column to 'Desert Island Birds': my eight all-time favourites. They were all birds that bring back special memories: Coot, Great Crested Grebe, Little Bittern, Swift, Blue-cheeked Bee-eater, Common Crane, Red-billed Tropicbird and Wandering Albatross.

I have been fortunate to have seen all these in the wild, but there are another 8000 or so species I have still not caught up with. So here is my wish list, the birds that I can only dream of seeing, some time in the future.

I have picked one bird from each of the world's eight great birding regions. My first choice, representing Europe, is Gyr Falcon, a bird that epitomises the stark beauty of the frozen north. To see it, I would travel to Varanger Fjord at the northern tip of Scandinavia, one of Europe's last truly wild places.

Crossing the pond to North America, I would love to join the forthcoming expedition in search of the Ivory-billed Woodpecker. Last seen back in the 1980s, this huge black-and-white bird is now almost certainly extinct, though there is just a chance that a pair or two may be clinging on in the swamps of Louisiana.

Alternatively, I could head for Cuba, where Ivory-bills have also been reported in recent years. If I failed in my quest, the consolation prize would be my third choice, Bee Hummingbird. At less than 6cm long, and weighing just 1.8 grams, this Cuban endemic is the smallest bird in the world.

For my fourth species, I would travel south to the world's most bird-rich continent, South America. With almost half the world's birds to choose from, it is not easy to pick just one, but the world's largest parrot, Hyacinth Macaw, would be hard to beat.

East now, to Africa. Last year we visited The Gambia on honeymoon, when the only disappointment was that we did not manage to see Carmine Bee-eaters. Of all the world's bee-eaters, this is arguably the most stunning, with its elegant shape, decurved bill and deep-red plumage.

My sixth and seventh birds both come from regions I have yet to visit: South-east Asia and Australasia. In Asia, the birds of paradise are unbeatable, and the one I would most like to see is the bizarre yet beautiful Wallace's Standardwing. Australasia is full of equally unusual birds, including a stunning range of parrots, kiwis and the amazing lyrebird. But I would travel a little further, to New Zealand's South Island, to look for the Takahe. This giant relative of the Moorhen was once thought to be extinct, until it was rediscovered in a remote valley during the 1950s.

For my eighth choice, I shall simply pick the next new species I see, whatever it is. Whether I am in Britain or some distant corner of the globe, seeing any new bird is always a thrill. And knowing that there are well over 8000 species out there I haven't seen is the only motivation I need to go out and look for them.

Car park birding

 OCTOBER 2000

I know it's not the sort of thing you're supposed to admit in the *Guardian*, but I like car parks. Please don't misunderstand me. I'm not talking about the multistorey variety or those vast concrete spaces at out-of-town shopping centres. My favourite car parks are in rather more rural settings: at places such as Stodmarsh, Titchwell and Minsmere, some of Britain's best-known hotspots for birds.

The reason is simple. Sometimes the best views are those you get the moment you open your car door, or when you're about to turn the key in the ignition and leave. It may be the constant presence of human activity, but birds in car parks often seem tamer and allow closer views, than those on the actual bird reserves.

Last November, my partner Suzanne and I went out for a Sunday afternoon walk at Stodmarsh, in the Stour Valley in Kent. The car park was full of bird activity, with flocks of Goldcrests and Long-tailed Tits foraging in the surrounding bushes, calling to each other as they went. In contrast, the reserve itself was deathly quiet. Six months later, at exactly the same place, a Cetti's Warbler competed with a Wren and a Whitethroat to see who could sing loudest. No prizes for guessing that the Cetti's won.

If you want to catch up with another loud songster, the Nightingale, just visit Minsmere in the last week of April or the first week of May, and stand on the edge of the car park. You'll soon hear the song of the poets' favourite bird, and if you hang around long enough, you have a good chance of seeing it as well.

Another RSPB car park, at Pulborough Brooks in Sussex, provided me with fabulous views of a nesting Nuthatch. I was leading a beginners' birdwatching course for the Field Studies Council, during a particularly wet spring weekend. As the rain finally stopped, the bird popped in and out of its nest hole, just a few feet above our heads.

Supermarket car parks can be just as good for birds. Flocks of Ring-necked Parakeets regularly fly over the Richmond branch of Waitrose on their way between the River Thames and Richmond Park, while Asda, on the Norwich ring road, occasionally plays host to flocks of Waxwings, winter invaders from the north.

But these are eclipsed by the rarest bird ever seen in a supermarket car park: Britain's first and only Golden-winged Warbler, discovered next to Tesco's in Maidstone, back in February 1989. This tiny bird, hardly bigger than a Blue Tit, had presumably arrived from North America the year before, swept across the ocean by autumn gales. Why it chose to make its home in such unusual surroundings we'll never know, but it was much appreciated by a crowd of several thousand avid twitchers. Unfortunately, I never got around to seeing it.

The magic of car parks works on the other side of the pond, too. This spring we visited Cape May, North America's finest spot for migrating songbirds. At least, that's what we were told. In fact, migrants were few and far between, but one did perform beautifully: a fine male Prairie Warbler, singing its heart out in, yes, the car park.

And my most memorable car park sighting? Probably the flock of Tristram's Grackles at En Gedi, Israel, last January. These sooty-black birds were drinking from a leaky hose, the only fresh water for miles around. When startled by a car horn or engine, they would fly a short distance, revealing bright orange linings to their wings, before returning to their little oasis in the sand.

The Great Escape

MARCH 2001

Sixty years ago next month, a young man began observing the breeding behaviour of a pair of Redstarts. With the help of friends and colleagues, he continued doing so for four years, amassing a wealth of data. Then, the Second World War came to an end, and he never saw his beloved birds again.

The man was John Buxton, and his studies took place at a German prisoner-of-war camp called Eichstätt, deep in the forests of Bavaria. Eichstätt was an ideal place to study birds, and as a prisoner for more than five years, he had plenty of time to do so. As author Peter Marren has observed: 'In some ways, prisoner-of-war camps offer rather good opportunities for birdwatching. It is hard to imagine any other circumstances in which so many intelligent, active people would have so much spare time on their hands, nor so much incentive to find a distracting pastime.'

Buxton cut an unlikely figure as an ornithologist. In fact he was not a professional scientist at all, but a tutor in English literature at Oxford. But when he was imprisoned in Eichstätt, after his capture during the ill-fated Norwegian campaign, he began to look around for something to alleviate the boredom, and the Redstarts fitted the bill.

So while his fellow inmates spent their time dressing up as chorus girls or digging escape tunnels, Buxton turned his attention to the study of Redstarts. He immediately enlisted help, organising his colleagues with military efficiency. Regular observations began in April 1941, and soon took up virtually all the prisoners' free time. In just three months, from April to June 1943, Buxton and his team spent a total of 850 hours watching the birds – an average of more than nine hours a day.

Buxton was acutely aware of the irony of his situation, as a captive man watching free birds: 'My redstarts? But one of the chief joys of watching them in prison was that they inhabited another world than I; and why should I call them mine? They lived wholly and enviably to themselves, unconcerned in our fatuous politics . . .'

After the war, Buxton returned to academia, and was later active in promoting bird ringing, introducing the mist-net into Britain from Germany. He died in 1989, virtually unknown to the modern generation, but mourned by all those who remembered him. As a legacy he left a delightful monograph in the Collins New Naturalist series, *The Redstart*, now sadly out of print.

John Buxton was not the only birdwatcher at Eichstätt. The camp also played host to a young advertising executive named Peter Conder, who had been captured in June 1940, and like Buxton spent five long years in the prison camp. His captors got so used to his birdwatching activities that he became a useful look-out during escape attempts. He made detailed observations on Goldfinches, recording his results on whatever material was available, including German toilet paper.

Conder's experience was quite literally a life-changing one. After the war, instead of returning to a career in advertising, he became warden of Skokholm Bird Observatory off the Welsh coast. Later, he became director of the RSPB, increasing its membership tenfold during his time in charge. Thus the man who described himself as 'an academic failure, and a bit of a loner' became one of the leading conservationists of his day: all thanks to some Goldfinches – and a plentiful supply of toilet paper.

Keep out!

 APRIL 2001

So, the countryside is closed. Or to put it more accurately, most places where people normally go to watch birds are currently not open to visitors. Birdwatchers all over Britain are confined to seawatching, reservoirs or a walk round their local park. But the situation is not quite as bad as it may seem. Birdwatchers may be frustrated, farmers devastated, and the tourism industry tearing its hair out. But for the birds, at least, the foot-and-mouth crisis may turn out to be a good thing.

Britain is a very crowded island. Our 120 million or so birds have to share their space with almost 60 million humans, along with their dogs,

cats, bicycles and cars. Whether we mean to or not, we cause disturbance to birdlife. Dog-walkers flush breeding partridges and Skylarks;
mountain bikers and off-road vehicles carve up nesting habitats; and
birdwatchers themselves sometimes disturb the very birds they come
to see.

Not now, though. With much of the countryside out of bounds to
the casual visitor, birds can get on with their lives more or less undisturbed by humans. In London's Richmond Park, for instance, Skylarks
and other ground-nesting birds can look forward to a bumper breeding season, without the unwelcome attention of dog-walkers and their
pets. Numbers of predatory crows in the park have also declined dramatically, because the lack of human visitors means less rubbish and
waste food for them to scavenge. Elsewhere, in the 'real' countryside,
the clock has been turned back to a time when the only human presence
was the local farmer.

Of course, birds do not live in an ecological vacuum. Indeed, many
species that breed on moorland or farmland depend on the annual cycle
of grazing by sheep or cattle, which provides suitable habitat for breeding and feeding. If these animals disappear from large swathes of the
countryside it will not only be a disaster for the farmers but could also
bring problems for birds like the Lapwing that make their nests on
grazing land.

Incidentally, in their search for a scapegoat for the current crisis
some sectors of the media have decided to put the blame on birds. It is
not beyond the bounds of possibility that birds can spread the disease,
but given the sorry state of intensive farming that led to the crisis in the
first place, it does seem a bit like shooting the messenger.

Meanwhile, the countryside is at last beginning to open up to visitors, albeit in a fairly limited way. Some RSPB reserves, such as
Titchwell Marsh in north Norfolk or Radipole Lake in the heart of
Weymouth, are open and will provide many people with a welcome
birding fix over the next few weeks.

As for the future, what will be the long-term effects of foot-and-mouth disease on Britain's birdlife? One thing is sure: never before has the countryside been put under so much scrutiny. Once the crisis is over there is likely to be a radical rethink of agricultural policy, hopefully resulting in a return to more traditional, wildlife-friendly ways of managing the land. If and when this happens, we can only hope that the needs of our birds are recognised, along with those of farmers, tourists, birdwatchers and everyone else with a vested interest in the British countryside.

Where have all the birds gone?

 MAY 2001

A few years ago, an American ornithologist wrote a book with the provocative title *Where Have All the Birds Gone?* He showed that North America's songbird population had undergone a drastic decline since the Second World War, mainly as a result of habitat loss and modern farming methods.

I am tempted to write a book of the same name today. For over the past few years, along with many others, I have begun to notice declines in many once familiar birds. Last week I was in north Norfolk, hoping for a range of spring migrants and newly arrived summer visitors. True, the weather was hardly ideal – persistent north-easterlies for the whole three days – but I was still surprised at the lack of birds. At Cley, the only migrant waders were a small party of Ruffs and the odd Whimbrel, while Titchwell was hardly any better. Songbird migrants were thin on the ground, too: with just a few Whinchats, although one of these was in the same binocular view as a day-flying Barn Owl.

Which brings me to the good news: some birds are clearly increasing in numbers. Barn Owls, Sparrowhawks and Marsh Harriers are all regular sights on a trip to Norfolk nowadays, whereas when I first visited the county in the 1970s they were scarce. Avocets are thriving, too: a welcome boost for the RSPB.

A few days later, on May Day Bank Holiday, I visited Dungeness. There, too, there were good numbers of some birds, including plenty of Sedge Warblers and Whitethroats, and a heavy passage of Swallows and Swifts. But it has been years since I regularly saw birds like Bullfinches, Willow Tits and Lesser Whitethroats, which in my youth were fairly common. The latest *London Bird Report* reveals the seriousness of the decline, with the Willow Tit, once a regular breeding bird in the capital, down to just seven individuals, none of which bred.

Whatever the cause of these declines (and they are probably due to a combination of factors), one thing is clear: by and large, birds which live on reserves, such as Avocets and Marsh Harriers, are doing fine, while birds with wider but sparser distributions, including farmland and woodland species, are declining – in some cases perhaps even heading towards extinction.

That may sound a bit over the top. But recent studies have suggested that when bird populations decline they do not do so in a neat and orderly fashion. Once numbers drop below a certain level, whatever conservation measures are put in place, the species may be doomed.

Take the Passenger Pigeon. Once the commonest bird in the world, it was so abundant that flocks containing tens of millions of birds literally darkened the North American skies as they passed. The birds were shot indiscriminately for food, and a rapid decline began. For some reason, the pigeons appeared to lose the will to breed, and numbers dropped like a stone. Fifty years later, in 1914, the last surviving Passenger Pigeon, Martha, died in captivity in Cincinnati Zoo.

Nothing so dramatic has ever occurred on this side of the Atlantic. But when we start to notice the decline of familiar birds such as the Song Thrush, Starling and House Sparrow, it's time to get worried. So next time you hear that songbird populations are in decline, don't console yourself with the thought that they will recover. This time, there's just a chance that they might not.

Two for joy

 APRIL 2003

I've always had a soft spot for Magpies, not least because they featured in the very first article I ever wrote for the *Guardian*, a dozen or so years ago. These splendid birds are, for most people, part of the landscape – especially if, like me, you live in a leafy suburb, packed with trees and gardens.

And packed, of course, with garden birds. For there's the rub. In the bird world, Magpies are currently vying with Sparrowhawks as public enemy number one, because of their tendency to prey on the eggs and chicks of some of our best-loved songbirds.

Since the end of the Second World War, Magpies have undergone a population boom and recolonised many areas from which they used to be absent. This is due partly to the drop in numbers of gamekeepers, who would shoot Magpies on sight and ask questions afterwards. During roughly the same period, several species of songbird have suffered dramatic declines – some, like the Song Thrush and House Sparrow, to the point at which we are seriously worried about their future. Many people have, understandably, put two and two together and made five. To them, Magpies are the evil villains responsible for our songbirds' demise.

But things are not quite as simple as they might seem at first sight. In fact, Magpies are not the culprits. Yes, they do take eggs and chicks – though even at the height of the breeding season these still only make up about a third of their diet.

Let's look at it another way. If Magpies are responsible for the decline, why did songbirds not die out centuries ago? Why are so many garden birds doing rather well? And most importantly of all, what do the species that have declined most rapidly have in common? Not that they are predated by Magpies – but that they feed for much of the year on seeds.

The seed-eaters – birds like the Tree Sparrow, Linnet and Corn Bunting – have declined more than any other group. When I was a child the bird books classified these as 'farmland species' – though few do so now. That's because on many arable farms you would be lucky to find a spare seed in winter, let alone come across the stubble fields filled with birds that I remember from my youth.

So who is to blame for the decline in songbirds? Top of the list are farmers – at least those who embraced modern, high-intensity farming methods and took the subsidies that went along with them. They are closely followed by consumers of cheap supermarket food – who went along with an agricultural policy that left no room for the birds. Does that sound familiar? Well, that category certainly includes me – and probably you too.

Max & Guy

MAY 2003

In the autumn of 1926, a young man named Max Nicholson went up to Oxford. His subject was history, but his passion was birds, and he soon joined the newly formed Oxford Ornithological Society. In contrast to the hedonistic behaviour of the 'Brideshead Set', with their endless round of parties and costume balls, the ornithologists were an earnest bunch. Instead of propping up the college bar and getting 'hog-whimperingly drunk', they were often out from dawn to dusk making careful observations of bird behaviour.

But today, almost 80 years later, the achievements of these pioneers have lasted far longer than those of their pleasure-seeking contemporaries. In 1928 Nicholson and his fellow birdwatchers carried out the first-ever survey of a breeding bird, the Grey Heron. During the following three-quarters of a century Britain's birds have been surveyed, counted and watched more than any other comparable avifauna in the world. We still have a lot to learn, but much of what we do know is down to the vision and lifetime's work of Max Nicholson.

Sadly, Max died last month, just over a year short of his own century. I was fortunate to meet him several times, and always felt as if I were travelling back in time. He would refer to some of the greatest figures of twentieth-century ornithology as 'young Peter Scott' or 'that young fellow James Fisher'. He would casually mention 'a book I wrote in 1926' or the time he met Edward Grey – Britain's longest-serving Foreign Secretary, author of *The Charm of Birds*, and the man who coined the famous phrase: 'The lights are going out all over Europe; we shall not see them lit again in our lifetime.'

Max lived a full and varied life outside ornithology, too: as private secretary to Herbert Morrison, and with Churchill at the postwar peace conferences at Yalta and Potsdam. He also told me of a visit to the remote islands of St Kilda, inspiring me to go and see this remarkable place for myself.

Most movingly of all, he talked of his memories of 1914, when as a ten-year old boy in Portsmouth he watched the columns of young men going off to war. As we now know, so many of them were never to return. This tragedy shaped the entire course of his life, making him determined to make up for their loss by helping to create a better world. As the father of modern conservation he certainly did his best.

In the same week as the passing of Max Nicholson, another colossus of twentieth-century ornithology also died. Guy Mountfort had packed almost as much into his 97 years. He led the first great birding expeditions to Europe, told in his inspiring series of *Portrait* books; was co-author (with Roger Peterson and Phil Hollom) of the legendary *Field Guide to the Birds of Britain and Europe*; and set up Operation Tiger, which helped prevent the extinction of this magnificent beast.

Max Nicholson and Guy Mountfort were truly great men, who fought against the destruction of the world's wildlife and inspired succeeding generations to do so too. But for me, their most important legacy is their simple enthusiasm for watching birds. For all their work

on committees and at conferences, organising expeditions and writing
books, neither Max nor Guy ever forgot one thing – that ultimately we
watch birds for the joy and pleasure they give us.

A trip with Tono

 JUNE 2003

As I was reading the obituaries of Max Nicholson and Guy Mountfort
in this month's *Birdwatching* magazine, a brief paragraph caught my
eye. It announced the death of another, less well-known figure in the
birding world. Less well-known, perhaps, but just as sadly missed.

At 77 years old, Jose Antonio Valverde was a generation younger
than the two British nonagenarians, but their lives were nevertheless
closely linked. As a young man in the late 1950s, 'Tono', as he was
known, was the only Spanish ornithologist on Guy Mountfort's pioneering expeditions to the Coto Doñana in southern Spain – Europe's
last great wilderness.

He made an immediate impression, both for his deep knowledge of
local birds and his patchy command of English. On one occasion, he
and James Ferguson-Lees were out horse riding when they heard a
strange sound. Unsure of its identity, Ferguson-Lees asked Valverde
what was making the noise. Struggling for the correct word, Valverde's
face suddenly brightened, and he pronounced his verdict: 'Adult
tadpole'!

As a child, I remember reading about this adventure in the great
bird photographer Eric Hosking's autobiography *An Eye for a Bird*,
and wondering if I might ever get to visit the magical Coto Doñana for
myself. In 1986, almost 30 years after the first expedition, I finally did –
in the company of Tono Valverde.

At the time I was making a BBC television series teaching Spanish,
and a colleague had tracked him down for me. He let us into his tiny

apartment, a broad smile on his kindly, suntanned face. The conversation soon turned to my interest in birds, and Valverde's eyes lit up. To my astonishment, he grabbed his car keys and announced: 'Vamos! Let's go to Doñana!'

We left Seville in his battered car, stopping every few miles to scan the skyline with a pair of borrowed – and equally battered – binoculars. But Valverde was not happy. It was clear that intensive agriculture was ruining a unique habitat. Much of what had once been natural wetland, formed by the flooding of the Rio Guadalquivir, had been drained, ploughed and planted with crops. In an absurd irony, the authority responsible for this damage, the European Union, was simultaneously financing a project to pump water back into the damaged land.

Finally, however, we reached a crossroads, overlooking a vast area of water covered with wildfowl and wading birds. As the sun set, Valverde told me the story of how Doñana had been saved for posterity by the newly formed World Wildlife Fund. He recalled drinking a bottle of wine to celebrate, then in a minor act of eco-vandalism, throwing the bottle into the water to commemorate their victory.

As if on cue, two Greylag Geese and two Greater Flamingos flew past in formation across the glowing sky. Valverde watched them pass and said in a quiet voice: 'Geese and flamingos. North meets south. That is why this place is so special.' Later, he presented me with an inscribed copy of his book on the Coto Doñana, which I still treasure to this day.

The following year, I was in Seville once again and received a message from Valverde inviting me to go with him to look for vulture nests in the Andalusian mountains. The birth of my first son was imminent, however, and I had to decline his offer and return home to England. I greatly regret that I never went birding with Tono Valverde again.

My favourite bird

 MAY 2004

This year, I saw my first Swift on 21 April, a week or so earlier than usual. As always, it was a moment that defines the coming of summer and makes me realise that the natural world is still functioning as it should. Others, including former Poet Laureate Ted Hughes, have shared this view. He once penned these lines on the birds' miraculous annual return:

> They've made it again,
> Which means the globe's still working, the
> Creation's
> Still refreshed, our summer's
> Still all to come . . .

But what is it about Swifts that inspires us so? Well for a start, their ability to fly here non-stop from Africa, homing in on the urban sky-scape that will be their summer home. Then, once they get here, their extraordinary morning and evening display flights, as dozens of them chase each other across the sky like racing drivers entering a chicane, screaming as they go. It was this extraordinary sound that earned them the folk name 'devil bird', along with dozens of other related epithets including 'devil screamer', 'swing devil' and even 'devil's bitch'.

Yet despite their association with Satan, most people regard Swifts with affection and admiration rather than fear. This may be because if you live in the centre of a city, the Swifts' arrival is often the first indication that the long dark days of winter are finally over, and summer has finally begun.

I also like to think that we recognise athletic prowess when we see it. For as their name suggests, Swifts are the ultimate flying machines: capable of staying airborne for months on end, sustaining themselves by grabbing small insects in their huge gapes as they fly.

They even sleep on the wing. Watch as dusk falls on a fine summer's evening, and you will see the Swifts rise higher and higher into the heavens, eventually disappearing from view. It is here, high in the sky, where they choose to rest: though catnapping might be a better description.

For such an aerial bird, landing is the exception rather than the rule. Indeed the only time Swifts perch at all is when they visit their nest, usually under the eaves of a tall building. One of the most famous colonies is in Oxford, where they breed, appropriately enough, in the tower of the university's Museum of Natural History. Half a century ago, the great Oxford ornithologist David Lack wrote about this colony in his book *Swifts in a Tower*, still one of the best popular scientific accounts of a British breeding bird.

But as Lack noted, if a Swift lands on the ground, it is in big trouble. Aerodynamically designed for flight, with huge wings and tiny legs (its generic name *Apus* actually means 'no feet'), once the bird is accidentally grounded it finds it almost impossible to get airborne again.

I remember getting a phone call many years ago from a friend's mother, who had discovered a Swift on her back lawn after a heavy thunderstorm. When I arrived the bird was a shivering mass of dark feathers and looked close to death. But we picked it up and dried it off, then as the rain cleared, took it outside to be released. I can still remember the feeling of joy as I watched it take off from my outstretched palm and fly off into the grey skies, back where it belonged.

Why watch birds?

 JUNE 2004

Gardeners have always known about the therapeutic value of their hobby; now, it seems, they can be even more pleased with themselves.

For they are not only healthier and happier than their counterparts without green fingers, they actually live longer as well.

The fact that close encounters with plants makes for a well-balanced way of life comes as no surprise to me. The same is true, after all, of anyone with a passion for nature. Over the years I have come to know a very varied bunch of wildlife enthusiasts, and although they come from a wide range of backgrounds, they have one thing in common: a zest for life. It is easy to assume that this comes from being out and about in the fresh air, maintaining their physical fitness, but there is much more to it than that. In my view, the mental, emotional and spiritual sides of wildlife watching are at least as important as any physical benefit.

Talk to anyone who has gone through a major life-changing event – redundancy, divorce or bereavement, for example – and ask them how they came to terms with the change in their lives. Of course, family and friends are the first people you turn to, but if you have a passion for watching wildlife you have another vital means of support.

At its most basic, nature offers you a way to escape. In times of crisis, being able to get away from it all is a great help, and you are probably better taking a country walk than drowning your sorrows in the local pub. Then there is the sense of perspective you get from wildlife. Watching a wild animal go about its daily business really does put human affairs into context. It helps you realise that whatever is happening to you, the world is still turning and other living things are carrying on with their daily lives.

If you have a local patch – a place where you regularly go to watch and enjoy wildlife – then you are in touch with the passing of the seasons, and the comings and goings of birds and other creatures. In a world where it is all too easy to get things out of context, this is by far the best way to re-engage with reality.

Seven years ago this spring my mother died, and soon afterwards my marriage broke up. From being confident, happy and successful I was plunged into a mood of doubt and despair. Fortunately I had the support of my friends and family, and the love of my life, Suzanne. But I also had a place to think, to reflect on life and to escape.

Now, I can look back on that difficult time with something approaching equanimity. And I can take my young son Charlie around my local patch and point out the birds – though being just seven months old he has not quite learnt how to use binoculars yet. As we watch fox cubs gambolling on the grassy bank, listen to the chorus of marsh frogs and enjoy the antics of nesting Lapwings, I can affirm that being close to nature really does make you feel better.

Year listing – a century on

DECEMBER 2004

One hundred years ago, on 1 January 1905, a young man living on the borders of Kent and Sussex decided to keep a list of the number of different birds he saw on New Year's Day. Horace Alexander only managed 17 species, so the following year he enlisted his brother Christopher in the quest. This time they were more successful, tallying a grand total of 33.

Looking back almost seven decades in his autobiography *Seventy Years of Birdwatching*, Horace Alexander recalled how relaxed he and his brother had been. They did not even leave the house until after breakfast, returned home for lunch and travelled everywhere on foot.

But a tradition had begun, and despite excuses, hangovers and the call of the January sales, thousands of birders will keep it going on 1 January 2005. Why we do so is hard to explain: but there is something about the freshness of the New Year that brings hope to the heart of even the most jaded birder.

In North America, this obsession with listing finds its outlet over the whole of the festive season. The Christmas Bird Count began in

1900, when a young ornithologist named Frank Chapman persuaded about two dozen people to go out and log not just the species they saw, but the number of individual birds as well. Nowadays the Christmas Bird Count is a national tradition: with 2000 different events involving about 50,000 participants, from Alaska to Hawaii and California to Florida. Counters use every possible method to log birds, including dog-teams, canoes, hang-gliders, hovercraft and even golf-carts!

At the BBC Natural History Unit, we indulge in a rather more leisurely contest, organised by my colleague Martin Hughes-Games. With a silver cup at stake, the birders among us count the total number of species we see during eight days, from midnight on Christmas Eve to the end of New Year's Day. In the past, some contestants have considered sending themselves on a filming trip to some exotic location in order to snatch the prize, but this was thought to be contrary to the spirit of the contest, and all participants must now remain within the borders of the UK.

Attitudes to the contest vary between the laid-back and the fanatical. Some people hire cottages on the north Norfolk coast to be as near to the birds as possible, while others have the advantage of living near Chew Valley Lake, with its wintering Bitterns. If you want to win, an early start is essential: last year one participant heard both Tawny and Little Owls during the first half an hour after midnight – despite, as he put it, being 'very, very drunk'.

True to the amateur ethos of the contest, I shall take a couple of walks around my local patch, gaze out of the back window and tick off Ring-necked Parakeet – safe in the knowledge that this exotic creature has not yet reached Bristol, where most of my colleagues live. Horace and Christopher Alexander would, I am sure, have approved.

The hit list

 JUNE 2006

A few years ago, I wrote about my all-time favourite birds in this column. Now it's time to come clean and give you the top five birds I could, to put it politely, do without. If my choice upsets you, I apologise, but sometimes you just have to get things off your chest.

At number five on my list, Meadow Pipit. Not that there's anything offensive about this little bird; just that, as the archetypal 'little brown job', it defines the word 'nondescript'. Sometimes you catch a glimpse of an odd-looking bird out of the corner of your eye and imagine for a brief moment that it is something rare and interesting. Almost always, it's just another Meadow Pipit.

At number four, Greenfinch. Actually it was a toss-up between this and Herring Gull, but as so many people have a downer on gulls I feel it behoves me to stand up for them. So Greenfinch it is. Maybe it's that annoying wheezy call or the fact that they monopolise bird feeders most of the year round, but I just can't get that excited about them.

At number three, Wood Pigeon. Surely I must mean Feral Pigeon, the famous 'rats with wings'? In fact Feral Pigeons are amazing birds, with an extraordinary history, having mutated from the wild Rock Dove into the ultimate city slicker we know today. The Feral Pigeon has been scandalously ignored both by professional ornithologists and amateur birders, with the honourable exception of Eric Simms, whose book *The Public Life of the Street Pigeon* taught us most of what we know about them. So instead I have gone for the Feral Pigeon's big brother, the Wood Pigeon. There's just something about these birds that annoys me – I'm sure they do have interesting habits, but they are just too big and gaudy for my liking.

At number two, and jostling for the top spot, is Greylag Goose. The late Konrad Lorenz, who pioneered the study of animal behaviour known as ethology, would doubtless disagree, but this bird is surely the most aesthetically challenged of all our native birds. It used to make up for this deficiency by living in remote and beautiful parts of Scotland, but in the past couple of decades there has been a boom in the feral Greylag population, and today it can be found all over the place, still looking gormless.

And which species occupies the coveted number one spot in the league table of birds I wouldn't miss if they disappeared tomorrow? I'm afraid it's another goose species, and this time I'm not alone in my choice. Canada Geese may look good as they migrate south from their native home, filling the air with their haunting cries, but their presence on virtually every pond, lake and river in the country is a crime against nature. It's not just that they are foreign – I have often admitted a soft spot for the equally alien Ring-necked Parakeets – but that they simply have no redeeming features, and enough unpleasant habits to fill a book. If only they were good to eat . . .

Remembering George Montagu

 JULY 2006

Of all the people who have influenced the history of birdwatching, my personal favourite is the eighteenth-century ornithologist George Montagu. He was the first to classify several British species, including the bird that still bears his name – Montagu's Harrier.

Yet for the first forty years of his life Montagu had very little to do with birds. Instead, he pursued a career path typical of men of his class and background: joining the army and reaching the rank of lieutenant-colonel, before settling down with his wife and six children in his home county of Wiltshire.

Despite his worldly success, Montagu was a deeply frustrated man. A few years earlier, he had written to his mentor Gilbert White, confessing that he had 'delighted being an ornithologist from infancy and, was I not bound by conjugal attachment, I should like to ride my hobby into distant parts . . .'

In 1799, he got his wish. Having begun an affair with a married woman, he was court-martialled and forced to leave military service. He and Eliza, his mistress, headed down to Kingsbridge in Devon, and spent the rest of their lives watching, cataloguing and writing books about birds. Not a bad result from what nowadays we might call a mid-life crisis.

I thought of George Montagu when, on the way back from a recent birding trip, I called in at a secret site where a pair of Montagu's Harriers was nesting. I say 'secret', but the birders' grapevine is more efficient than most, and at least a dozen people were waiting for Britain's rarest bird of prey to appear.

Normally, when hoping to see such a special bird, I spend a fruitless hour or two gazing into the distance, before giving up and heading home. 'You should have been here yesterday' is a sentence I have heard more times than I care to remember.

But not this time. Barely five minutes after I arrived, a shout went up from one of the watchers, and I focused my telescope on a bird on the horizon. It was a male 'Monty' in all its splendour: almost falcon-like on its long, narrow, pale-blue wings. Slimmer and more elegant than other harriers, a Montagu's shares their ability to cruise low over the ground, with a buoyant and seemingly effortless flight action.

As the male approached the nest the female flew up to meet it. Larger than her mate, she also has a very different plumage: mainly chestnut-brown, with a narrow white rump. The male was carrying food, and sure enough, they flew into the sky and performed the 'food-passing' ritual that cements their pair-bond — as well as providing the sitting female with much-needed nourishment. Two Marsh Harriers came over to investigate, but were promptly chased away by the male. After checking that there was no other imminent danger, he flew off into the strengthening northerly breeze, a vision of beauty and grace.

CHAPTER 7

Back home

2001–PRESENT

Things came full circle in August 2001, when Suzanne and I moved to Hampton: the place I went to school, and just a few miles down the road from where I grew up. This time it took me a little longer to find a new local patch, but when I did, it proved to be even more varied and enjoyable than the previous one. In two years I recorded just short of a hundred species and enjoyed some memorable experiences, some of which are documented in this chapter.

I also discovered the joys of truly local birding: our modest suburban garden is in a great position to attract a wide range of visitors and fly-overs, and when a Song Thrush turned up recently we had finally totted up 50 species here. Mind you, when I lived round here in the 1960s and 1970s there was a Song Thrush singing from almost every rooftop – proving that not all change has been for the better. The real star of our garden avifauna is the controversial Ring-necked Parakeet – and I have to admit that I love them, screeching and all.

The biggest life-change during this period has been the arrival of three children in rapid succession: Charlie in November 2003, and George and Daisy just 15 months later. No wonder my birding has been largely restricted to gazing out of the back window!

Now, as this book goes to press, we are planning our biggest move of all: from suburban London to rural Somerset. We're going to live in that mysterious place – half land, half water – known as the Somerset Moors and Levels. That's 'moor' in the sense of 'Moorhen' – meaning mere, or shallow lake. To paraphrase Noel Coward: 'Very wet, Somerset'.

Although I'll miss this area, I can't help thinking that the richness of the birds and other wildlife down in Somerset will compensate for no longer being woken at dawn by a squadron of parakeets screaming overhead. Over the coming years, I plan to report on the birdlife of my new local patch in the pages of the *Guardian*.

Until then, here is some more familiar fare . . .

Welcome back to Hampton

OCTOBER 2001

If you asked most birders how their interest first began, they would probably say it was from watching birds in their garden. According to a recent RSPB survey, two out of three people in Britain regularly feed garden birds. Many of them also keep a list of what they see. The rules are simple: any bird which either lives in, visits or flies over your garden can be counted, providing you can see it from somewhere on your property.

So when we moved home in mid-August, we had barely begun to unpack before we started off our new garden list: with a Collared Dove perched on the roof. After six weeks or so, the total stands at 34 species: pretty good for a small suburban garden on the outskirts of west London.

Our new home is in Hampton, very close to the River Thames. The proximity of the river, together with some small reservoirs, makes the local birdlife much more exciting. Every evening hundreds of Black-headed Gulls stream overhead on their way to roost, along with smaller numbers of the larger gulls and a few Cormorants.

Being on a flight-line, as this is known, brings all sorts of surprises. On our first evening, as we sat outside on the patio, a flock of Mistle Thrushes passed overhead – no doubt coming from nearby Bushy Park, where they feed during the day. A Grey Heron, Kestrel and Sparrowhawk have also made occasional appearances.

But the one bird that really makes its presence felt is the latest arrival to the local avifauna. Regular as clockwork, at dawn and dusk, flocks of Ring-necked Parakeets appear, shattering the peace and quiet with their noisy calls. We have seen groups of up to 30 birds, presumably heading for their roost at Esher Rugby Club, just across the river. These so-called 'aliens' are now firmly established as a British breeding bird.

The best sighting so far occurred in early September, on the day of our house-warming. As guests gathered in the back garden, I looked up at the flocks of House Martins gathering overhead. High above them, dark against the blue sky, was a familiar, streamlined shape: a Hobby. Thirty years ago, when I first came to school in Hampton, this would have been an extraordinary record. Nowadays, following a population boom, Hobbies are a fairly regular sight over the west London suburbs. No less exciting for that, though.

Unfortunately, so far very few birds have graced our garden with their presence. Although we have put up several bird feeders, the only birds to venture within our boundaries are a couple of Blue Tits and a noisy, but elusive Wren. One of the problems is that the charming family next door owns two cats, which regularly prowl around our garden in search of food.

If the cats ate spiders, they would be well satisfied, for these are the most prominent inhabitants of our garden. So we can only hope that in the coming months, as food gets scarcer, a few more birds will be tempted to visit. Meanwhile, as the chill winds of autumn begin to blow, and the House Martins head off to warmer climes, I look forward to some more surprises from our local birds.

A surprising visitor

 JANUARY 2002

It's a cloudy, dull Sunday in the middle of January, and I'm looking out of my window. A Magpie chases another across the sky, a Wood Pigeon perches in a tree, and over the distant peal of church bells, I can hear the calls of Jackdaws as they pass overhead.

Yesterday, as I looked out of the same window, a flock of tits passed through the garden: constantly calling to one another as they hopped to and fro, before launching themselves onto a feeder to grab a single sunflower seed at a time. The day before that, I heard a Blackbird calling. Looking across the roof of the neighbour's garage, I saw a movement in a bush – a small, greyish-brown bird with a milk-chocolate-coloured crown. It was a female Blackcap, feeding voraciously on juicy berries before flying off to seek sustenance elsewhere.

Three snapshots of the birdlife from my window, in a typical London suburb. Nothing out of the ordinary, you might think. Except that by the time you read this, some of those small birds might have died through lack of food. Another could have been killed by a cat. On the bright side, the Blackbird may have begun to sing, staking out his territory for the coming spring.

For however ordinary the birds you see from your own window, it's worth remembering that from a biological point of view the struggle they face is no different from that of any wild creature. Take the Blackcap. This little bird, weighing barely as much as a pound coin, was born in central Europe, probably last year or the year before. In the autumn, along with its siblings and parents, it headed in a north-westerly direction towards Britain. After crossing the North Sea it ended up here, by the River Thames in Hampton, where a mild winter's climate and plenty of food give it a better than even chance of surviving the winter.

Even more extraordinary, this Blackcap is one of the best examples of evolution in action. Thirty years ago her ancestors migrated south-west, to spend the winter in Spain or North Africa. Then, by some random genetic mutation, a small proportion of the German Blackcap population began to head off in a completely different direction.

In normal circumstances they would have perished and that would have been that. But because this random mutation conferred some tiny evolutionary advantage, they survived and returned to breed. Little by little, the process of natural selection increased the proportion of these birds in the general population. A couple of decades later, and they have taken over. Today the whole of this population of Blackcaps spends the winter in Britain and Ireland.

For scientists, this is doubly fascinating. First, it shows the speed with which natural selection can act on living creatures. Second, it lends weight to the notion that our environment is changing as a result of global warming. The recent unprecedented run of mild winters – together with food provided by us – has enabled these Blackcaps to survive.

So next time you look out of your window, don't just take the birds you see for granted. Every one of them has an extraordinary life history, is worth watching, and will repay the benefit of close study.

My new local patch

The Cuckoo shot across the island as if fired from a gun, hotly pursued by a frantic pair of Lapwings. Veering round, it passed right in front of the West Hide, giving wonderful views. Like all unexpected sightings, it produced a mixture of thrill and satisfaction. First, a shot of adrenaline as I realised this was something different; then, the excitement of watching it at close quarters; finally, as it disappeared, the satisfaction of having seen a new bird for the site. For this was not Cley, Minsmere or Stodmarsh, but a little nature reserve on the suburban outskirts of west London. Welcome to my new local patch.

For seven years back in the 1970s, I took the train each day from Shepperton to school in Hampton. Along the way we passed some reservoirs at Kempton Park, though I don't recall taking all that much notice of them. Thirty years later, Thames Water has turned one of these into a nature reserve, sandwiched between the racecourse, some allotments and a housing estate. Initial impressions are not very inspiring: first, you negotiate a narrow, muddy path favoured by dog-walkers and horse riders; then you go through what look like the gates to Colditz, presumably designed to keep out local vandals.

But if you shut your eyes and listen for a moment, the experience takes on a much more pleasant feel. As soon as you leave the road you are serenaded by the local Blackbirds and Robins; further along the path the sound of Chiffchaffs and Blackcaps begins; and as you walk up the grassy bank towards the hide, Whitethroats and Willow Warblers add their voices to the chorus.

On my very first visit, back in March, the highlight was the view from the West Hide. From its lofty vantage point on the banks of the old reservoir, I looked down upon a stage filled with frantic activity. Coots and Moorhens were building their nests, Great Crested and Little Grebes were diving for food, and the air was filled with the calls of Lapwings as they fought off every intruder, including Jackdaws, crows and foxes, with a brave and noisy assault.

Since that first visit I have been back at least a couple of dozen times. There have been unusual sightings, such as a Buzzard flying lazily overhead on a bright spring morning; a Bar-tailed Godwit which stopped to feed for a few days on its way to the Arctic; and a male Garganey posing in front of the hide one evening in early May. But even when only the usual birds are present, there is always something to enjoy: from displaying Whitethroats to the pugnacious antics of the Canada Geese. And like all local patches, there is always the chance of something unexpected turning up, like that Cuckoo.

After that first sighting, we strolled round to the East Hide, and had no sooner settled down when we spotted the Cuckoo again. He was sitting on a bush, feeding on hairy caterpillars, and giving fabulous views. We watched, enthralled, as he used his beak to remove the poisonous innards of the caterpillar before wolfing it down his throat. Not something I expected to see when I set out from home, an hour or so before.

Natural rhythms

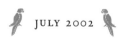

JULY 2002

My mother always used to say that when you buy a new house, you should live with the garden for a year or so before you make any major changes, so that you truly understand its seasonal rhythms.

A local patch is a bit like that. When I first visited Kempton Nature Reserve back in March, spring was just around the corner, and the last few wintering ducks and waders could still be seen. Soon afterwards, summer visitors began to appear, and by the third week of April all four common warblers – Chiffchaff, Blackcap, Whitethroat and Willow Warbler – were singing constantly from dawn to dusk. The next week saw the first House Martins, while my birthday on 26 April coincided with the arrival of those true sentinels of summer, Swallows and Swifts.

May was full of goings-on, the highlights being a fine male Garganey and a female Bar-tailed Godwit, both on their way north to breed. It always amazes me when a bird just drops in for a rest on its way from Africa to Scandinavia or the Arctic, but that's just one of the things that make a local patch so special.

May was also a time of frantic breeding activity: first, courtship and nest-building, then egg-laying, and finally the miraculous appearance of dozens of baby birds, which seemed to be everywhere. The most notable breeding species here are Little Ringed and Ringed Plovers, with their larger relative the Lapwing, whose frantic cries mean the place is rarely quiet.

June continued in the same vein, with some chicks growing bigger by the day, while other, less fortunate, ones met an early demise through predatory crows or foxes. The foxes, too, have provided plenty of interest, whether swimming across to the island on yet another egg raid or simply playing with their cubs on the path near the hide.

As the year goes on, the wildflowers have grown too: so that the path is now a bit of a jungle. Weeds produce seeds, so I'm not complaining – and neither are the Goldfinches and Linnets which have already arrived to feed. I've even seen a pair of Bullfinches, though they are often elusive – something which can't be said for the many broods of Blue, Great and Long-tailed Tits flitting around the bushes.

Now it's July, which in the birders' calendar means the start of autumn. Small flocks of gulls have begun to turn up, much to the distress of the local Kestrel, who mobs them whenever they get too close. Last week I saw my first Dunlin for the reserve, probably a returning migrant heading back south for the winter. Hopefully this will be the first of many migrating waders dropping in to feed during the next few weeks.

So with less than a third of the year gone by since my first visit, I am beginning to understand the nature of the place: who lives here, who drops in from time to time to feed, and who just passes through on their way somewhere else. I've enjoyed the comings and goings of more than 75 different kinds of bird – and missed at least a dozen more. In the global, or even the national, sense, Kempton Nature Reserve may not be particularly important, but from a local point of view, it's priceless. Like most people, I spend most of my time near where I live – so for me, this is one of the most important places of all.

Half-term report

OCTOBER 2002

It's six months since I began visiting my new local patch, Kempton Nature Reserve – so it's time to give the place a half-term report. Overall, it has more than lived up to my expectations, though as with any new location, there are birds which I didn't expect to see, but have; and those which I did expect to see, but haven't – at least not yet.

For some species in the latter category, it can only be a matter of time. As summer gives way to autumn, I'm sure that a Great Black-backed Gull will drift overhead soon, while Goldcrests, Redwings and Fieldfares must also be on their way. I only saw my first Mistle Thrush last week, while other recent additions include Pheasant, Wigeon and Pochard. I was surprised not to see any Sedge Warblers this spring, and missed out on Lesser Whitethroat, Redstart and Yellow Wagtail, all of which were noted by other observers.

Nevertheless, my current total of 84 species (out of 97 recorded at the site this year) is not too bad, considering that I only started in March. My aim is to reach a personal total of 100 species by the end of next year – a daunting, though far from impossible task.

Of those 84, what were the highlights? It is always tempting to pick out the unexpected visitors – one-offs like the Bar-tailed Godwit that stayed for a few days in late April, the Cuckoo in June or the Little Egret in August. But although birds like these always set the pulse racing, a local patch is really about the regular species – and the subtle changes that occur as the weeks and months pass by.

At the time of my first visit, in late March, the first spring migrants had yet to arrive. By early May, the place had been transformed into a cauldron of birdsong, with residents and summer visitors competing for airspace. In mid-May, the young birds began to appear – dominated by ducklings, goslings and cygnets. Things quietened down a bit in June and July, though as the chicks grew larger the amount of squabbling increased. August saw an influx of Teal and Lapwings – with six new additions to the 'patch list' including Hobby, a bird I had managed to miss on several previous occasions.

The driest September for a long while has reduced the water levels considerably, and the past couple of weeks have been very quiet. There have been a few surprises, such as a new brood of Little Grebes, and one evening, a flock of a couple of hundred Jackdaws flying overhead. These must have come from their feeding grounds in Bushy Park, on their way to roost – but who knows where? They certainly showed no signs of landing as they continued westwards.

Meanwhile, Jays have just begun to arrive in good numbers, while the tit flocks, so quiet during late summer, are active again. Sound-wise, the spring chorus has given way to a single soloist – the Robin and its delightful autumn song.

In many ways, sights and sounds like these are the most satisfying thing about regularly visiting a local patch. During the next six months bird numbers will build up for the winter – and although the variety of species will no doubt decline, there will be the spectacle of hundreds of ducks, gulls and Lapwings. Something to look forward to as the long autumn nights draw in.

Sunny afternoon

 AUGUST 2003

On the hottest day ever recorded, with the thermometer finally breaking the 100-degree barrier, the best place to be was the garden. But by early evening, as the temperature finally began to drop, I decided to take a walk around my local patch.

This long, hot summer has played havoc with the breeding birds: low water levels mean that just one pair of Lapwings has raised chicks, while the usual Ringed and Little Ringed Plovers have long since vanished. The Mute Swans have three healthy cygnets, and the chatter of Little Grebes is constant, but apart from the odd Robin or Dunnock there are few signs of young songbirds. I fear that it has been a poor breeding season all round, as seems to be the case all over the country.

To compensate for the lack of bird activity, I have been paying more attention to butterflies and dragonflies. Butterflies are also thin on the ground this year, though I usually see a Speckled Wood along the path, while Gatekeepers and Meadow Browns flit around the sunnier areas of the reserve. I've seen several Banded Demoiselles, identified by their distinctive wing pattern, and on the few remaining patches of water, the larger hawkers and Emperors cruise around like fighter pilots looking for the enemy.

Nevertheless, there are still a few birds to see. Some don't worry about the heat, and there are plenty of Wood Pigeons and Stock Doves feeding on weed seeds on the sides of the reserve. Goldfinches, too, are plentiful – hanging onto thistles to extract the precious seeds. Some are juvenile birds, lacking the red face patch of their parents, giving them a rather baffled expression.

August is usually the time when a migrant or two drops in, but in the fine weather many seem to be passing overhead without landing. One exception is the Green Sandpiper, a couple of which have stopped off on their long journey south to Africa. It is one of the joys of birding at your local patch that birds like this, which breed no nearer to Britain than Scandinavia, pop in on their migratory travels across the globe.

Meanwhile, some of our own summer visitors are already on their way. We are still seeing the odd Swift over the garden, but most have now headed off to Africa, while numbers of House Martins are also beginning to drop. Soon it will be autumn, and it will be left to the resident birds to keep up the interest. On this particular visit, the star performer was a female Sparrowhawk, which pounced on an unwary Starling right in front of the hide where I was sitting.

Contrary to popular belief, Sparrowhawks do not always dispatch their prey with a single blow. So as the unfortunate Starling continued to struggle, she attempted to pin it down with her powerful talons. This activity soon attracted interest, and as the Sparrowhawk tried to pluck the feathers from her prey, she had to fend off the unwelcome attentions of a Magpie and a couple of young crows. Eventually, fed up with the interference, she flew off, the Starling still held tightly in her grasp.

A charming little bird

 MAY 2005

'A charm of Goldfinches' is not a phrase you hear very often these days, but the collective noun for this delightful little bird could not be more appropriate. For of all our native songbirds, the Goldfinch has a good claim to be the most attractive and endearing.

When we moved to south-west London four years ago, we had all the usual garden birds to visit. Blue Tits and Great Tits, Greenfinches and Chaffinches, even the odd Ring-necked Parakeet would drop in to take advantage of our seed and peanut feeders. But for the first year or so, we saw no Goldfinches.

Nor did we hear them. For the first sign that you have Goldfinches in the neighbourhood is usually their sound: a tuneful, tinkling call often uttered in flight. But despite my best efforts, our garden and its surroundings remained resolutely Goldfinch-free.

Then, after a year or so, I tried a different strategy. I bought two new bird feeders: one, a monstrous metre-long creation of metal and plastic, which I filled to the brim with sunflower hearts. The second, a smaller and more modest affair, containing a special product called nyger – tiny, black, grain-like seeds which are reputed to attract Goldfinches as cheese attracts mice. I must admit that I was fairly sceptical. For a start, the tiny holes on the sides of the feeder looked too small to allow any bird to extract the contents. But I decided to give it a go, and so with my two new feeders primed for action, I retreated to the sitting room.

What I am about to tell you may make you think I am exaggerating. But it is the honest truth that within an hour I heard the telltale tinkle from the skies above, and there, on my nyger feeder, was a pair of Goldfinches. Minutes later, they were joined by another, and another, until a whole flock was enjoying a free lunch.

It was then that I realised that I had underestimated both the bird and the designer of the feeder. For the Goldfinch is the only species with a bill thin and pointed enough to be able to extract the tiny seeds from the slightly less tiny holes. Greenfinches give it a go but give up in frustration. Starlings and House Sparrows simply do not stand a chance.

Since then, we have enjoyed the presence of Goldfinches on virtually a daily basis, with flocks of a dozen or more regularly appearing. Sometimes, I take a closer look through the binoculars I keep by the back window and never fail to marvel at the sheer beauty of their plumage. Subtle shades of beige and cream; black wings emblazoned with the flash of yellow that gives the species its name; and the bright crimson face – said to be the result of the Goldfinch attempting to remove Christ's crown of thorns and becoming wounded in the process.

And even when I don't see them, I can hear that bubbling call as they fly overhead. A call that reminds me that in our eagerness to seek out the rare and exotic, we can all too easily overlook the common and familiar. For the Goldfinch is, in every sense of the word, a charming little bird.

Out of the woods

 APRIL 2006

On a fine spring evening – and there haven't been many of those so far this year – I love to sit on the little patio at the back of our house and listen to birdsong. By April the chorus is well under way, with the tinkling notes of the Goldfinch, the delicate tones of the Robin and the impossibly energetic trill of the Wren all competing for my attention. But the sound that I most enjoy hearing is the leader of the orchestra: the fluty tones of a male Blackbird, belting out his song as if his life depended on it.

Which in many ways, it does. For this bird certainly isn't singing purely, or even partly, for my benefit. His song may be beautiful – and may have inspired generations of poets, musicians and writers – but that Blackbird perched on the nearby roof is engaged in a battle as serious as any in the natural world. Before the summer is over, he must win a mate, fend off rivals to his territory and raise as many young as he can. The race to reproduce is on – and given that most songbirds only live for a year or two, this may be his last chance.

This springtime battle is at its most intense in my suburban neighbourhood, here on the outskirts of London. Studies have shown that town Blackbirds breed at densities up to ten times greater than their country cousins. So, even as I listen to 'my' Blackbird, I can hear an answering song from two or three others nearby. The reason for this incredible breeding success is that gardens are ideal for Blackbirds to nest and raise a family: providing plenty of food, places to nest and song-posts from which they can serenade the neighbourhood.

Yet it goes without saying that these built-up areas are not the Blackbirds' original habitat. Like so many of our garden birds, they evolved as creatures of woodland, living in the dense, leafy canopy and feeding on the forest floor. Only in the past couple of centuries have they discovered that our towns and cities, with their leafy avenues and intensively managed gardens, provide the perfect place to feed, drink, rest and nest. They moved in and have never looked back.

But like all living creatures, Blackbirds cannot hide their evolutionary origins. Even if they no longer lived in woodland, we would know that they originally came from there, for one simple reason: their song. Those deep, fluty tones, which make its song so appealing to the human ear, must have evolved to allow the sound to carry as far as possible through the dense foliage. Leaves soak up high-frequency sound, but the deep, baritone notes of the Blackbird penetrate this green barrier, allowing my bird's ancestors to defend their territories and win mates.

Not that any of this concerns the fine male Blackbird sitting on the roof opposite me and keeping a close lookout with that beady, black eye. Once he is happy that I present no immediate threat, he relaxes, opens his beak and sings, to his – and my – heart's content.

Charlie and birds

 AUGUST 2005

At almost two years old, my son Charlie has already mastered the art of identifying some of our common birds. Hardly surprising, really. After all, when I brought him back from hospital when he was just two days old, one of the first things I did was to hold him up against the window and show him the birds on our garden feeder.

His first bird? A Goldfinch – one of my favourites, and I hope someday one of his. Since then I have taken every possible opportunity to point out birds, and he has learnt to identify 'dove' (a category that includes Wood Pigeon as well as Collared Dove); 'parrot' (the ubiquitous and noisy Ring-necked Parakeets) and 'Robin' (almost any small bird). If he fails to identify a particular species, he can always fall back on the general category of 'bird', which includes every living thing to visit our suburban garden, apart from the odd cat or squirrel.

My greatest achievement so far has been to teach him the identity of my favourite British bird. Earlier this summer we spent a very pleasant week in the Dorset market town of Beaminster, whose old houses support a healthy population of low-flying Swifts. After a day or two of me pointing them out as they whizzed overhead, Charlie finally got it. From that moment on, every small bird flying across the sky is, to give it his distinctive pronunciation, a 'wift'. Even if it's a House Martin. Or indeed any other species.

All very charming, but will it make him interested in birds as he grows up? Some might consider that with two parents already converted, he has little choice in the matter. But I am not sure whether you can 'teach' a passion like birding or whether there is some kind of innate factor that makes someone gravitate towards birds, as opposed to, say, music or sport.

With my older two sons, now in their teenage years, I opted for a softly-softly approach. The result was that they have never taken more than a passing interest in birds, to put it mildly. So this time I have decided to be a pushy parent. Given that Charlie already has two younger siblings, six-month-old George and Daisy, I am hoping that at least one of them will follow in my footsteps.

But why am I so determined to get my children interested in birds and birding? Is it just so I can have someone to carry my telescope on long walks or talk to in my old age? I would like to think that I have a more altruistic motive. For I have gained so many benefits from my passion for birds – both professionally and personally – that I would love my children to share in the joy of birding.

Soon I shall be getting them their first bird book, then a pair of binoculars. In a few years we will go on trips to bird reserves, where they can annoy the 'serious' birders in the hides by talking too loudly. Eventually, I hope, I shall instil in them a passion for birds – and indeed other wildlife – that lasts their whole life long.

Epilogue

MAY 1997

My mother was never really interested in birds. But she still encouraged me in my new-found hobby. At first, this meant trailing after me and my classmate Roger, as we walked around the local gravel-pits in search of Great Crested Grebes. I can still remember the excitement when we finally saw a pair of these beautiful birds.

Family holidays were spent at Milford-on-sea in Hampshire. This was close to the wonderful Keyhaven Marshes, where for the first time in my life I watched wading birds such as Oystercatchers, Redshank and Dunlin.

But things got really serious when, for my thirteenth birthday, I became the proud owner of a pair of Carl Zeiss binoculars. My first chance to try them out came at Minsmere, where my mother sat patiently in hide after hide as I marvelled at the Avocets, Marsh Harriers and multitude of other birdlife at that fabulous reserve.

1974 was, I suppose, my *annus mirabilis*. That summer, I cycled off to the New Forest on a camping trip with my friend Daniel, blissfully unaware of my mother's terror at letting her only child go off on his own at the tender age of 14. Somehow we managed to survive unscathed, although on reflection, I wouldn't let my own children loose on the roads at that age.

That September, she took me to the Isles of Scilly, even allowing me two weeks off school, to the outrage of my teachers who for some strange reason thought that O-levels were more important than autumn migration.

Our final birding trip together came the following summer, when we visited the hills and valleys of mid-Wales in search of Choughs, Dippers and the magnificent Red Kite. I particularly remember one hot August Sunday, when we drove for miles and miles along steep, twisting roads, stopping every now and then to scan the skies for this rare and elusive creature.

We were just about to give up, when I noticed a Buzzard flying overhead. As I glanced through my binoculars, a second, smaller bird passed by in the blue sky above. My first Red Kite, and one that I've never forgotten. We decided to celebrate with a visit to a local pub, but had forgotten that in those days, most of Wales was 'dry' on a Sunday. The pub was well and truly shut. I don't think my mother ever forgave them.

That trip was the end of an era. By now I no longer needed my mother's services as a chauffeur and guide, and I was old enough to travel on my own. Following university, I joined the BBC, and earlier this year fulfilled a long-held ambition by producing a television series on birdwatching, *Birding with Bill Oddie*. My mother was overjoyed and telephoned every one of her friends and neighbours to tell them the good news.

I last saw my mother on a fine, sunny afternoon in early April. We sat in her back garden in Shepperton, listening to the singing of Greenfinches, while the sparrows raided the peanut feeder. A week later, while I was on a birdwatching trip to Jordan, I heard the news. My mother had died, suddenly, of a heart attack.

It is impossible to put into words how you feel about the loss of a parent. But after the grief and the sorrow, comes the gratitude. Thanks to her early encouragement, I have enjoyed the benefits of a lifetime's passion for birds and birdwatching. Now, I'm passing on her legacy to my younger son, James, who carries his granny's binoculars on our regular Sunday morning birdwatching trips.

So mum, for all this and for much, much more, thank you.

Acknowledgements

For some, birding is a solitary activity; for others, including me, a sociable one. As a result, the list of people I should like to thank for their companionship, guidance and support is a long one. To each of the individuals mentioned here, I am truly grateful.

My late mother, Kay Moss, without whom I might never have become interested in birds in the first place; the forgotten relative who bought me *The Observer's Book of Birds*; my teacher in form 2H, Saxon School, Mrs Threlfall; my classmates Alan Higgs, Glyn Goodwin, Rob Lightowlers, Ian Hyde and Roger Trent; Robert Elliott (YOC leader); the late Dr Drew Thompson, who kindly lent me his Zeiss binoculars; the late Bert Axell; Daniel Osorio, my longest-standing birding companion; his parents David and Martine Osorio; Nick Riddiford; Mick Lane; Franco Maroevic; the late Alan Turner; Ron Bloomfield; Neil McKillop; Sacha Barbato; Jo Hemmings; Mark Golley; David and Marta Sharrock; Suzanne Levy; Anthony Wood; Simon Ware; Andrew McClenaghan; Bill Oddie; Clive and Audrey Byers; Graham McAlpine; Anne Varley; Mike Toms; Chris Skinner; Chris Knights; Nick Watts;

everyone for whom Lonsdale Road Reservoir was 'their patch'; the late Violet Hoare; Sam Moloney; Tim Appleton and Martin Davies; Tony Marr; Jackie Follett; Juliet Rix, Rod Standing and their sons Daniel and Luke; Nigel and Cheryle Redman; Rob Childs; John Aitchison; Chris Watson; Rita Aspinall; Lucy Meadows; the crew of the *Silurian*; Fiona Pitcher; Chris and Barbara Kightley; Richard Porter; Martin and Barbara Woodcock; Nick and Judy Comer-Calder; Mike Dilger; Robin Riseley; Scott Tibbles; Andy Hawley; Martin Hayward-Smith; Bill Pranty; Hadoram Shrihai; Chris and Helen Padley; the late Peter Grant; Killian Mullarney; Steve Rooke; Jucha Engel; Dan Alon; Barak Granit; Qusay Ahmad; Derek Moore; Gerard and Oda Ramsawak; Kenny Calderon; Susan Ramrattan; the production team and crew of *Big Cat Diary*; the staff of Governor's Paradise Camp, especially Colin Wellensky; Arnoud van den Berg; Richard North; Tim Hunt; the late Graham Hearl; Marek and Hania Borkowski, Nigel Bean; Richard Crossley; Pete Dunne; Sheila Lego; Marleen Murgitroyde; Joan and David Sibley; Pat and Clay Sutton; Ib Huysman; Solomon Jallow and Bubacarr Daffeh; the crew of the *Kapitan Dranitsyn*; Michaela Strachan; Ruth Flowers; Dirk Harmsen; Shireen Aga and Barbara Walker; Adam Chapman; Lena and Haffstein, the Eider farmers of Flatey; Dr Aevar Petersen; Debra Love Shearwater; Rob Yeoman; John A. Burton; David Cottridge; Steve Roberts; the late Jose Antonio Valverde; Cristina Lago; David Wilson; Eileen Goodwin; Martin Hughes-Games.

At the *Guardian*, I should also like to thank Celia Locks for her editing skills over the past 13 years or so, and for her relentless war against my occasional tendency to make the column read like a Christmas round-robin letter! Also at the *Guardian*: Tim Radford, Stephanie Kerstein, Bernard Hunt and Martin Page. And not forgetting my friend and former colleague Paul Simons, whose generous suggestion that I joined him in writing the *Guardian's* Weather Watch column originally led to my association with that newspaper.

I owe great thanks to all those involved in the production of this book, including designer Peter Ward, copy-editor Wendy Smith and

Managing Editor at Aurum Press, Phoebe Clapham. The doyen of British bird artists, Robert Gillmor, provided the delightful and striking cover illustration, while Jan Wilczur did the line-drawings that grace each chapter. As always my dear friend Graham Coster (himself a birder of growing enthusiasm and distinction) did his usual excellent editing job. And of course to readers of this column past and present; thank you for your kind and supportive letters over the years. Here, at last, is the book so many of you have requested . . .

Finally, as always, I owe a huge debt to my family: my sons David, James, Charlie and George; my daughter Daisy; and my wife Suzanne, with whom so many experiences in this book have been shared. I look forward to many more in the future.

STEPHEN MOSS
Hampton, Middlesex; May 2006